CONVERSATIONAL FRENCH

MADE EASY

By

Monique Jackman**, B.A., Fr.Ed.T.C.**

HADLEY PAGER INFO

First Edition, 2005

ISBN 1-872739-15-6

Copyright Monique Jackman , 2005

Printed and Bound in Great Britain by Antony Rowe Ltd., Chippenham

HADLEY PAGER INFO
Leatherhead, Surrey, England

FOREWORD

Monique Jackman, B.A., is a French-born speaker who holds the Further Education Teacher's Certificate and has taught French to junior and adult students in Britain since 1978. She is author of four French learning packs (work sheets) for children aged 11-16 and is also author of "Speaking Better French" first published in 2000. The latter now entitled just "Better French" has proved highly popular and has been followed by a second edition and subsequent reprints.

Conversational French Made Easy is designed to help those who have a basic knowledge of French and wish to brush up and improve their conversational skills, and is therefore of particular value to advanced students of French aiming for a university degree, as well as to Brits who have newly moved to France and found their French rustier than expected.

In this book Monique has chosen over 120 French verbs, with two or more meanings, which are frequently used in conversation and has prepared multiple examples illustrating their usage in the context of their different meanings. Her teaching experience has shown that multiple examples of the spoken use of verbs is of tremendous value in learning their use in a fluent fashion and enables students rapidly to achieve confidence in their application in conversations.

The only secret to become fluent in French (or indeed any other language), as with other skills, is practice. No more, no less. This simple fact can not be overstressed. Speak, listen to, write, read French at every opportunity. The parallel translations in Conversational French Made Easy make working alone possible, as well as working in pairs, or in small groups of keen or willing family members and friends,

This book also functions as a verb dictionary since the various meanings are listed, however those meanings which are much less or seldom used in conversation are not provided with examples.

Also meanings are omitted of the following types:

- those that are not part of standard language and that should only be handled with care by non-native speakers in relaxed situations.
- those that are specialist French.
- set phrases (verb + verb, or verb + other word) as these could be far too many for a good number of the verbs.

The book also makes the differences between the two languages very clear. The use of bold type in the examples shows the

- different word order (especially with compound tenses) in negative and interrogative forms as well as with other words such as pronouns.
- different key structures needed , for example French active voice with 'on' as the subject instead of English passive voice.
- different tenses used to say the same thing.
- huge number of reflexive verbs in French, often used instead of the passive voice in English.

Finally for the academically minded a list of the infinitives and participles of each verb are given in an appendix.

ACKNOWLEDGEMENTS: Cover Picture: PARIS-PLAGE. Photograph by Catherine Balet. Courtesy of Paris Tourist Office ©.

Blank spaces in this book have been decorated with figures from the ancient world, courtesy of the W. Smith Collection. In sequence these are Danaids (p28), Dragon (p31), Artemis (p39), Hermes (p67), Alexander (p69), Atlas (p140), Calypso (p152), Philetaerus (p201), Charon, Hermes & Soul (p212), Paris (p224), Europa (p232), Eros on a Lion (p243).

CONTENTS

Former	Prendre
Fuir	Presser
Gagner	Rappeler
Garder	Rapporter
Gêner	Rattraper
Heurter	Recueillir
Ignorer	Récupérer
Importer	Regarder
Introduire	Régler
Joindre	Rejeter
Lâcher	Relever
Lancer	Remettre
Livrer	Remonter
Louer	Rendre
Marcher	Renverser
Mettre	Repasser
Mijoter	Reporter
Monter	Reposer
Noter	Représenter
Noyer	Retirer
Obliger	Retourner
Offrir	Revenir
Opérer	Rouler
Ordonner	Sauver
Parcourir	Sentir
Passer	Soulever
Placer	Tenir
Plaindre	Toucher
Planter	Traiter
Porter	User
Poser	Verser
Poursuivre	Voler
Pousser	

ABAISSER - S'ABAISSER

1 - To lower, to move down

- ➢ Il vaudrait mieux **abaisser** cet interrupteur. It would be better to **lower** this switch.
- ➢ J'**ai abaissé** l'antenne mais sans résultat. I **lowered** the aerial but it didn't make any difference.
- ➢ Qui **a abaissé** les étagères? Who **has moved** the shelves **down**?
- ➢ Que faut-il **abaisser**? What needs to be **moved down**?

2 - To reduce, to drop

- ➢ Elle **a abaissé** le loyer. She **reduced** the rent.
- ➢ Le niveau de la rivière **a abaissé** de plusieurs centimètres. The river **dropped** several centimetres.
- ➢ Le taux de naissances continue d'**abaisser**. The birth rate **is** still **dropping**.
- ➢ La population du village **abaisse/s'abaisse** rapidement depuis dix ans. The population of the village **has been dropping** fast for ten years.

3 - To pull/push down

- ➤ Vous **avez abaissé** les stores? **Did** you **pull** the blinds **down**?
- ➤ Je ne peux pas **abaisser** le couvercle de la boîte. I can't **push** the top of the box **down**.
- ➤ Elle lui **a abaissé** le col. She **pulled** his/her collar **down** for him/her.
- ➤ Tu peux m'**abaisser** cette petite branche? Can you **pull down** this small branch for me?

4 - To humiliate

- ➤ Nous nous sommes sentis **abaissés**. We felt **humiliated**.
- ➤ Je n'ai pas voulu l'**abaisser** devant ses amis. I didn't want **to humiliate** him/her in front of his/her friends.
- ➤ Il a dit qu'il allait l'**abaisser** à la première occasion. He said that he was going **to humiliate** him/her at the first opportunity.
- ➤ Ne **vous abaissez** plus comme ça. Stop **humiliating** yourself like that.

5 - To stoop

> Pourquoi **nous abaisser** à leur niveau? Why should we **stoop** to their level?
> Je n'ai aucune intention de **m'abaisser** à son niveau. I have no intention whatsoever **to stoop** to his/her level.
> J'espère qu'elle ne **s'abaissera** pas à un tel niveau. I hope that she **will** not **stoop** to such a level.
> Qui **s'abaisserait** à ce niveau-là! Who **would stoop** to that level!

6 - To bend down

> Attention à ta tête **abaisse-toi**! Mind your head **bend down**!
> Il **s'est abaissé** trop tard et il s'est fait mal. He **bent down** too late and he hurt himself.
> Je vais **m'abaisser** pour ne pas abîmer ma coiffure. I am going **to bend down** so that I don't spoil my hairstyle.
> Je l'ai vu **s'abaisser** pour mieux voir. I saw him **bend down** so that he could see better.

7 - To roll out (pastry).

ABOUTIR

1 - To succeed, to be successful, to have a successful conclusion/outcome

- ➢ Ça pourrait **aboutir** au résultat espéré. It could **succeed** as hoped.
- ➢ Ils méritent que leurs efforts **aboutissent**. Their efforts deserve **to be successful**.
- ➢ Il faut absolument que ces négociations **aboutissent**. It is vital that these negotiations **are successful**.
- ➢ Est-ce que les pourparlers **ont abouti**? **Was there a successful conclusion** to the discussions?

2 - To end up, to lead to (places)

- ➢ Ce boulevard **aboutit** au canal. This boulevard **leads** to the canal.
- ➢ La petite route **a abouti** à des champs. The little road **ended up** in some fields.
- ➢ Où est ce que ce chemin **aboutit**? Where does this path **lead** to?
- ➢ Si vous continuez tout droit vous **aboutissez** sur la grande place. If you go straight ahead you **end up** in the main square.

3 - To result, to have a result, to lead (to a result)

- ➤ Cela **a abouti** à un grand malentendu. It **resulted** in a big misunderstanding.
- ➤ Je pense que ça **aboutira** à un échec. In my opinion it **will have a** disappointing **result**.
- ➤ Tout cela n'**aboutirait** à rien. That **would lead** nowhere.
- ➤ Naturellement elle voudrait que ça **aboutisse** à quelque chose d'intéressant. Naturally she would rather it **led** to something worthwhile.

ACCEPTER - S'ACCEPTER

1 - To agree

- ➤ **Acceptez**-vous que vous aviez tort? **Do** you **agree** that you were wrong?
- ➤ Il n'**acceptera** jamais ça. He **will** never **agree** with that.
- ➤ Nous **avons accepté** de payer comptant. We **agreed** to pay cash.
- ➤ Elle **a accepté** de l'épouser. She **agreed** to marry him.

2 - To accept

- ➤ **As**-tu **accepté** l'invitation? **Did** you **accept** the invitation?
- ➤ Nous ne pouvons pas **accepter** ce comportement. We cannot **accept** this behaviour.
- ➤ Pourquoi ne veut-il pas **accepter** mon opinion? Why can't he **accept** my opinion?
- ➤ Ils n'**ont** pas **accepté** ma démission. They **did** not **accept** my resignation.

3 - To take on/in

- ➤ Pourquoi **as**-tu **accepté** cette responsabilité? Why **did** you **take on** this duty?
- ➤ J'**accepterais** de le faire volontiers. I would **take** it **on** willingly.
- ➤ Nous **acceptons** les animaux dans notre hôtel. We **do take in** pets in our hotel.
- ➤ L'asile **accepte** combien de sans-abri par nuit? How many homeless people **does** the shelter **take in** each night?

ACHEVER/ S'ACHEVER

1 - To end, to close

> L'année **s'est achevée** sous la neige. The year **ended** with snow.
> Heureusement tout **s'est achevé** dans une bonne ambiance. It all **ended** in a friendly atmosphere fortunately.
> Dès le discours **achevé** tout le monde s'est précipité au bar. As soon as the speech **ended** everyone rushed to the bar.
> La réunion **s'est achevée** sur une note triste. The meeting **closed** on a sad note.

2 - To finish

> Il **avait achevé** ses jours à l'étranger. He **had finished** his days abroad.
> **Avez**-vous **achevé** les travaux? **Have** you **finished** the work?
> Quand je suis entré elle **achevait** de s'habiller. When I went in she **was finishing** to dress.
> Il est parti sans **achever** son petit-déjeuner. He left without **finishing** his breakfast.

3 - To destroy, to kill

> ➤ Il a fallu **achever** le renard blessé. They had **to destroy** the injured fox.
> ➤ Une telle nouvelle pourrait l'**achever**. Such news could **kill** him/her.
> ➤ Le voyou est revenu une demi-heure plus tard pour **achever** sa victime. The thug came back half an hour later **to kill** his victim.
> ➤ Il avait cru avoir **achevé** son adversaire. He thought that he **had killed** his rival.

ADHÉRER

1 - To stick, to hold

> ➤ Malheureusement le papier peint n'**a** pas bien **adhéré**. Unfortunately the wallpaper **did** not **stick** very well.
> ➤ Les pansements n'**adhèrent** pas à une peau mouillée. Plasters don't **stick** on wet skin.
> ➤ Est-ce que la photo **adhèrerait** à cette surface? **Would** the photograph **stick** on this surface?

> ➤ Ma précédente voiture **adhérait** mieux la route que ma nouvelle voiture. My previous car **used to hold** the road much better than my new car.

2 - To support

> ➤ Nous n'**adhérons** guère à votre idée. We don't really **support** your idea.
> ➤ J'**ai** toujours **adhéré** à cette opinion. I **have** always **supported** this opinion.
> ➤ Elle **adhérait** à ce groupe depuis plusieurs années. She **had supported** this group for several years.
> ➤ Ils n'**adhèreront** jamais à ce parti. They **will** never **support** this party.

3 - To belong, to be a member, to join

> ➤ En **adhérant** à ce club on fait des économies sur les excursions. There are savings on trips out when you **belong** to/**are a member** of this club.
> ➤ Mes parents **adhèrent** à plusieurs associations caritatives. My parents **are members** of several charitable organisations.
> ➤ Pour **adhérer** il y a certaines conditions. There are certain conditions in order **to join/be a member**.
> ➤ Je ne pense pas qu'ils veuillent **adhérer** au syndicat pour le moment. I don't think that they wish **to join** the union just yet.

ADMETTRE

1 - To admit, to let in

> L'hôpital a-t-il pu **admettre** tous les blessés de l'accident? Was the hospital able **to admit** all the people injured in the accident?
> Je préfèrerais qu'on m'**admette** dans cette clinique. I would rather **be admitted** in this private hospital.
> Le club n'**admet** pas les enfants. The club does not **admit** children.
> Les chiens sont **admis** dans la plupart des restaurants en France. Dogs are **let in** most restaurants in France.

2 - To receive, to accommodate

> N'**admettez** personne dans cette pièce. Do not **receive** anybody in this room.
> Il voudrait qu'on **admette** cette jeune-fille dans notre foyer. He would like us **to receive** this young woman in our home.
> Je l'**ai admis** dans mon bureau. I **received** him in my study.
> Combien de personnes peuvent être **admises** dans cette salle? How many people can be **accommodated** in this hall?

3 - To pass (exams)

➢ Est-ce que tu **as été admis** au concours d'entrée? **Did you pass** the entrance examination?

➢ Malheureusement mon fils n'**a** pas **été admis.** Unfortunately my son **did** not **pass.**

➢ Aucun de nous n'**a été admis.** Not one of us **passed.**

➢ J'**avais été admis** de justesse. I **had** just about **passed** the exam.

4 - To accept

➢ Ils rêvent d'**être admis** dans ce collège. They dream about **being accepted** in this school.

➢ Combien de candidats comptez-vous **admettre?** How many candidates do you intend **to accept?**

➢ J'aimerais **être admise** dans votre entreprise. I would love **to be accepted** in your company.

➢ Sa candidature **a** finalement **été admise.** His/her application **was** finally **accepted.**

5 - To admit, to acknowledge

➢ Il lui faudra **admettre** qu'il a eu tort. He will have **to admit** that he has been wrong.

> ➤ Nous **admettons** que c'était la seule solution. We **admit** that it was the only solution.
> ➤ Est-ce que vous **admettez** que vous êtes responsable? **Do** you **admit/acknowledge** that you are responsible?
> ➤ Quand vont-ils l'**admettre**? When are they going **to admit/to acknowledge** it?

6 - To allow, to accept

> ➤ Elle n'**admet** pas qu'on fume dans les chambres. She does not **allow** smoking in the bedrooms.
> ➤ Est-ce que qu'ils **admettraient** ça ou non? **Would** they **allow** that or not?
> ➤ Pas question de l'**admettre**. It is out of question **to allow/to accept** it.
> ➤ J'**ai admis** la situation bon gré mal gré. I **accepted** the situation whether I liked it or not.

7 - To suppose, to assume

> ➤ **Admettons** qu'il vienne un autre jour. **Supposing** he came another day.
> ➤ **Admettons** qu'elles refusent. **Supposing** they refused.
> ➤ **En admettant** que nous ayons le choix. **Supposing/assuming** we had a choice.
> ➤ **En admettant** que vous ayez l'argent nécessaire. **Assuming** you had the necessary money.

AGIR - S'AGIR

1 - To behave, to act

- ➢ Vous **aviez** plutôt mal **agi**. You **had behaved/had acted** rather badly.
- ➢ Nous aurions dû **agir** d'une façon différente. We should have **behaved/acted** differently.
- ➢ N'**agis** plus comme un bébé. Stop **behaving/acting** like a baby.
- ➢ Elle ne sait pas comment **agir**. She does not know how **to behave/to act**.

2 - To act, to work

- ➢ Pourriez-vous **agir** dès que possible? Could you **act** as soon as possible?
- ➢ Ils ont décidé d'**agir** sans délai. They decided **to act** without delay.
- ➢ Il nous a fallu **agir** vite. We had **to act** very quickly.
- ➢ La pénicilline **a agi** tout de suite. The penicillin **worked** straight away.

3 - To work, to influence

> ➤ Est-ce que vos remarques **ont agi** sur elle? **Did** your remarks **work** on her?
> ➤ Rien n'**agit** sur lui. Nothing **works** on him.
> ➤ L'alcool **agit** sur les réflexes. Alcohol **influences** one's reflexes.
> ➤ Tu penses qu'elle saura comment **agir** sur eux? Do you think that she will know how **to influence** them?

4 - To be about

> ➤ **S'agit**-il simplement de temps? **Is** it only **about** time?
> ➤ Il ne **s'agira** jamais de ça. It **will** never **be about** that.
> ➤ Le problème dont il **s'agit** n'est pas d'hier. The problem it **is about** is not a new one.
> ➤ Il **s'agissait** de priorité. It **was about** priorities.

5 - What you/we have to do is

> ➤ Il **s'agit** de comprendre. **What you/we have to do is** understand.
> ➤ Il **s'agira** d'attendre patiemment. **What you/we will have to do is** wait patiently.
> ➤ Il **s'agirait** de les écouter. **What you/we would have to do is** listen to them.
> ➤ Il **s'agit** de leur pardonner. **What you/we have to do is** forgive them.

ALLER

1 - To go

- Où **va**-t-il? Where **is** he **going**?
- Nous **sommes allés** en France trois fois. We **went** to France three times.
- Ils **iront** ensemble. They **will go** together.
- **J'allais** à l'école à vélo. I **used to go** to school by bike.

2 - To be/go (health/life in general)

- Comment **vont** les chiens? How **are** the dogs?
- Il **va** mal depuis une semaine. He **has been** unwell for one week.
- Est-ce que le travail **va** aussi bien que possible? **Is** work **going** as well as possible?
- Comment **vont** les affaires? How **is** business **going**?

3 - To suit, to fit

- Ne te mets pas en colère ça te **va** pas. Don't get cross it doesn't **suit** you.

> ➤ Ça lui **va** vraiment bien cette casquette. That cap really **suits/fits** him/her.
> ➤ Ces lunettes ne me **vont** pas. These glasses don't **suit/fit** me.
> ➤ Cette jupe ne lui **va** plus. This skirt doesn't **fit** her anymore.

APPRENDRE - S'APPRENDRE

1 - To learn, to study

> ➤ **J'ai appris** à nager lorsque j'avais dix ans. I **learnt** to swim when I was ten.
> ➤ Il faut **apprendre** à conduire le plus tôt possible. It is best **to learn** to drive as soon as possible.
> ➤ Elle n'**a** jamais **appris** l'anglais. She never **learnt/studied** English.
> ➤ Qu'est-ce que vous **apprendrez**? What **will** you **study**?

2 - To hear

> ➤ Il **avait appris** ça la veille. He **had heard** it the day before.
> ➤ Vous **avez appris** la dernière nouvelle? **Have** you **heard** the latest news?

> ➤ Elle s'est évanouie en **apprenant** la tragédie. She fainted when she **heard** about the tragedy.
> ➤ Je ne veux pas qu'ils l'**apprennent** de quelqu'un d'autre. I don't want them **to hear** it from somebody else.

3 - To tell

> ➤ Il leur **apprendra** la vérité. He **will tell** them the truth.
> ➤ Je vais vous **apprendre** quelque chose d'intéressant. I am going **to tell** you something interesting.
> ➤ Nous venons d'**apprendre** qu'il est mort. We have just **been told** that he has died.
> ➤ Tu leur laisses le soin de lui **apprendre** ça? Are you leaving it to them **to tell** him/her?

4 - To teach

> ➤ Je vais t'**apprendre** à obéir. I am going **to teach** you obedience.
> ➤ Nous **avons appris** le français à des Anglais pendant plusieurs années. We **taught** French to English people for several years.
> ➤ On s'**apprendra** à jouer aux tennis. We **will teach ourselves** to play tennis.
> ➤ Ils souhaitent que j'**apprenne** le piano à leur fille. They want me **to teach** their daughter to play the piano.

APPUYER - S'APPUYER

1 - To press, to push

> ➤ Veuillez **appuyer** sur la sonnette avant d'entrer. Please **press** the bell before coming in.
> ➤ Il ne fallait pas **appuyer** sur ce bouton. You shouldn't have **pressed** this switch.
> ➤ **J'ai appuyé** ça. I **pressed/pushed** this.
> ➤ **N'appuyez** plus. Stop **pressing/pushing**.

2 - To lean, to rest

> ➤ Prière de ne pas **s'appuyer** sur ce mur. Please do not **lean** on this wall.
> ➤ Tu veux **t'appuyer** sur moi? Do you want **to lean** on me?
> ➤ **J'avais appuyé** l'échelle contre le pommier. I **had rested** the ladder against the apple tree.
> ➤ **N'appuyez** rien sur la clôture. Do not **rest** anything on the fence.

3 - To support

> ➤ Pourra-t-elle **appuyer** ta candidature? Will she be able **to support** your candidature?
> ➤ Mon patron m'a promis de m'**appuyer**. My boss promised **to support** me.
> ➤ Il est nécessaire d'**appuyer** vos observations avec des preuves. You need **to support** your comments with some evidence.
> ➤ Je suis surprise qu'ils n'**aient** pas **appuyé** ma demande. I am surprised that they **did** not **support** my request.

4 - To stress, to emphasize

> ➤ J'**ai appuyé** sur chaque mot exprès. I **stressed** every word on purpose.
> ➤ Ce n'est pas la peine d'**appuyer** ainsi sur ce fait. You don't need **to stress** this fact in this way.
> ➤ Nous aurions dû **appuyer** davantage sur les circonstances. We should have **emphasized** the position more.
> ➤ Il faudra **appuyer** sur cette dernière découverte. It will be necessary **to emphasize** this last finding.

5 - To do, to have to do, to put up with (a chore).

- ➤ Son mari **s'est** encore **appuyé** le repassage. Her husband **did/had to do** the ironing again.
- ➤ Ils **se sont appuyés** trois heures supplémentaires. They **had to do** three hours overtime.
- ➤ C'est toujours les mêmes qui **s'appuient** cette corvée. It's always the same ones who **do/have to do** this chore.
- ➤ Je n'ai nullement l'intention de **m'appuyer** tout ça tout seul. There is no way I am going **to do** all that on my own.

ARRACHER - S'ARRACHER

1 - To pull up/out, to take out

- ➤ Vous **avez arraché** toutes les carottes? **Did** you **pull up** all the carrots?
- ➤ Elle veut bien **arracher** les mauvaises herbes. She doesn't mind **pulling out** the weeds.
- ➤ N'**arrache** pas les fleurs coupe-les. Don't **pull out** the flowers, cut them.
- ➤ On lui **a arraché** trois dents. He had three teeth **taken out**.

2 - To tear off/out, to rip off/out

- ➤ Quelqu'un **avait arraché** une page dans l'agenda. Someone **had torn out** a page in the diary.
- ➤ Le vent **a arraché** le vieux toit. The wind **tore/ripped off** the old roof.
- ➤ Il **a arraché** son pantalon lorsqu'il est tombé du vélo. He **ripped** his trousers when he fell off the bike.
- ➤ Je viens d'**arracher** un bouton à ma veste. I have just **ripped off** one button on my jacket.

3 - To snatch, to grab (out of someone's hand)

➤ Un adolescent **a arraché** le sac d'une touriste allemande. A teenager **snatched** a German tourist's handbag.

➤ Il lui **a arraché** le journal. He **snatched** the newspaper from him/her.

➤ Tu n'avais pas besoin de me l'**arracher** des mains. You didn't need **to snatch** it out of my hands.

➤ Attention on dirait que le chien veut t'**arracher** ton sandwich. Careful it looks as though the dog wants **to snatch/grab** your sandwich.

4 - To drag (information) from/out

➤ Nous lui **arracherons** la vérité une fois pour toutes. We **will drag** the truth **from** him/her once and for all.

➤ Je suis sûr qu'il va essayer de t'**arracher** une décision. I am certain that he is going to try and **drag** a decision **out** of you.

➤ Il faut toujours tout leur **arracher**. You always have **to drag** everything **out** of them.

➤ Vous aviez l'intention de lui **arracher** son secret? Did you mean **to drag** his/her secret **out** of him/her?

5 - To tear (someone) away

- ➤ Comment vais-je pouvoir m'**arracher** à cette maison si intime? How am I going **to tear** myself **away** from this cosy home?
- ➤ Impossible de les **arracher** de la piscine. No one could **tear** them **away** from the swimming pool.
- ➤ Heureusement elle a pu s'**arracher** du malfaiteur. Fortunately she was able **to tear** herself **away** from the mugger.
- ➤ Il avait fallu **arracher** l'enfant des bras de sa belle-mère. They had **to tear** the child **away** from his/her step/foster mother's arms.

ARRANGER - S'ARRANGER

1 - To arrange, to organize, to fix

> Elle **arrangera** les rendez-vous. She **will arrange** the appointments.
> Je vous prie d'**arranger** une entrevue au plus tôt avec le client. Please **arrange** a meeting with the client as soon as possible.
> Tout **est arrangé** pour samedi. Everything **is organized** for Saturday.
> Qui **avait arrangé** la réunion? Who **had fixed** the meeting?

2 - To work out, to sort out

> On va essayer d'**arranger** ça. We will try **to work** it **out**.
> Je me demande si ça va **s'arranger** un jour. I wonder whether this is going **to work out/be sorted out** one day.
> Est-ce que votre situation **s'est arrangée** à la fin? **Was** your situation **sorted out** in the end?
> L'affaire délicate est loin d'être **arrangée**. The difficult question is far from being **sorted out**.

3 - To come to an agreement

- ➢ On a fini par **s'arranger** entre nous. We **came to an agreement** in the end.
- ➢ Est-ce qu'ils **s'étaient arrangés** ensemble? **Did** they **come to an agreement** between themselves?
- ➢ On **s'arrangera** comme on peut. We**'ll come to an agreement** the best we can.
- ➢ Voulez-vous **vous arranger** avec elle? Would you like **to come to an agreement** with her?

4 - To suit

- ➢ Cette date ne m'**arrange** pas du tout. This date does not **suit** me at all.
- ➢ A son avis ça les **arrangeait** de croire ça. In his/her opinion it **would suit** them to believe that.
- ➢ Tu ne viens que quand ça t'**arrange**. You only (ever) come when it **suits** you.
- ➢ Si vous pouvez changer l'heure ça les **arrangerait**. If you could change the time that **would suit** them.

5 - To arrange

- ➢ C'est notre fille qui **a arrangé** les fleurs pour la fête. It is our daughter who **has arranged** the flowers for the party.

- Les bibelots **étaient arrangés** sur l'étagère. The ornaments **were arranged** on the shelf.
- J'ai décidé de re-**arranger** les photos dans le salon. I decided to re-**arrange** the photographs in the lounge.
- C'est mal **arrangé**. It is badly **arranged**.

6 - To tidy up

- **Arrange** tes vêtements dans le tiroir s'il te plaît. **Tidy up** your clothes in the drawer please.
- Il est en train d'**arranger** sa tenue. He is **tidying** himself **up**.
- Il faut que j'**arrange** ma coiffure. I must **tidy** my hair **up**.
- Vous pouvez **arranger** les jouets sur le lit s'il vous plaît? Can you **tidy up** the toys on the bed please?

7 - To mend, to alter, to improve

- Est-ce que vous pourriez **arranger** ce manteau? Could you **mend/alter/improve** this coat?
- Comment est-ce qu'on va **arranger** la présentation? How are we going **to mend/alter/improve** the presentation?
- Nous **arrangerons** le texte un peu. We **will alter/improve** the text a little.
- Il l'**avait arrangé**. He **had mended/altered/improved** it.

ARRIVER

1 - To arrive, to come

- ➢ Ils **seront** déjà **arrivés**. They **will have** already **arrived**.
- ➢ Je **suis arrivé** à Paris mardi. I **arrived** in Paris on Tuesday.
- ➢ Nous n'**étions** pas encore **arrivés**. We **had** not **arrived** yet.
- ➢ Le car **arrivera** à quelle heure? At what time **will** the coach **come**?

2 - To reach

- ➢ L'eau de la piscine ne m'**arrive** qu'à la taille. The water in the swimming pool only **reaches** my waist.
- ➢ Est-ce que les lettres vous **sont** bien **arrivées**? **Did** the letters **reach** you all right?
- ➢ **Êtes**-vous **arrivé** à une conclusion? **Did** you **reach** a conclusion?
- ➢ Quand nous **serons arrivés** au bout de la rue nous nous reposerons un peu. When we **have reached** the end of the road we will rest a little.

3 - To succeed, to manage, to be able

➢ **Êtes**-vous **arrivé** à ouvrir le coffre? **Did** you **succeed** in opening the safe?

➢ Elles **sont arrivées** à lui faire comprendre. They **managed** to make him/her understand.

➢ J'espère **arriver** à tout faire demain. I am hoping **to manage/to be able** to do everything tomorrow.

➢ Personne n'**arrivera** à fermer cette fenêtre. Nobody **will be able** to shut this window.

4 - To happen

➢ C'**est arrivé** il y a une semaine. It **happened** a week ago.

➢ Que va-t-il leur **arriver** maintenant? What is going **to happen** to them now?

➢ Il ne m'**est** rien **arrivé**. Nothing **happened** to me.

➢ Qu'est-ce qu'il vous **arriverait**? What **would happen** to you?

ASSURER - S'ASSURER

1 - To assure, to promise

➤ Je vous **assure** que c'est la vérité. I **assure** you that this is the truth.

➤ Elle nous **a assurés** qu'elle l'avait fait de bonne foi. She **assured** us that she had done it in good faith.

➤ Tu m'**avais assuré** que tu ne le ferais pas. You **had promised** me that you wouldn't do it.

➤ Ils ne peuvent rien leur **assurer**. They can't **promise** them anything.

2 - To insure, to get insured

➤ Nous **assurons** notre appartement avec cette compagnie depuis vingt ans. We **have insured** our flat with this company for twenty years.

➤ **Avez**-vous **assuré** votre résidence secondaire? **Have** you **insured** your holiday home?

➤ Malheureusement il n'**était** pas **assuré**. Sadly he **was** not **insured**.

➤ Il faut absolument vous **assurer**. You really must **get insured**.

3 - To provide

- ➤ Son organisation **assurera** son logement. His firm **will provide** his accommodation.
- ➤ Un car de courtoisie **assure** le trajet à partir de l'aéroport. A free coach **is provided** from the airport.
- ➤ Mon travail n'**a** jamais **assuré** des véhicules de société. Company cars **have** never **been provided** where I work.
- ➤ Ce service n'**est assuré** que pendant l'été. This service **is** only **provided** in the summer.

4 - To ensure, to make sure

- ➤ Je vais **m'assurer** qu'il n'y a aucun problème. I am going **to ensure/to make sure** that there are no problems at all.
- ➤ Il ne **s'était** pas **assuré** que la bougie était éteinte. He **had** not **made sure** that the candle was put out.
- ➤ **Assure-toi** que tout est fermé à clé une dernière fois. **Make sure** that everything is locked one last time
- ➤ Je préfère **m'assurer** qu'ils sont bien rentrés. I would rather **make sure** that they got in safely.

5 - To secure

> ➤ Il ne pourra pas t'**assurer** un emploi dans son bureau. He won't be able **to secure** a job for you in his/her office.
> ➤ Il **a été assuré** de leur soutien. He **secured** their support.
> ➤ C'est un placement qui nous **a assuré** un revenu raisonnable. We **secured** a reasonable income from the investment.
> ➤ Son emploi leur **assurera** une retraite aisée. His job **will secure** a comfortable retirement for them.

6 - to steady (oneself, things).

AVANCER - S'AVANCER

1 - To move forward, to bring forward, to put forward

- ➤ Les animaux ne veulent plus **avancer**. The animals don't want **to move forward** anymore.
- ➤ Je l'ai vu **avancer** la main. I saw him **put** his hand **forward**.
- ➤ **Avancez-vous** un peu s'il vous plaît. **Move forward** a little please.
- ➤ La date **a été avancée**. The date **has been brought forward/has been put forward**.

2 - To approach

- ➤ J'aimais regarder les bateaux **s'avancer** vers le port. I used to enjoy watching the boats **approaching** the harbour.
- ➤ Les soldats **s'avançaient** vers l'ennemi sous une pluie battante. The soldiers **were approaching** the enemy in heavy rain.
- ➤ Elle **s'est avancée** vers les deux dames suspectée de vol à l'étalage. She **approached** the two ladies suspected of shoplifting.
- ➤ Le camion **s'avance**? **Is** the truck **approaching**?

3 - To put forward, to suggest

> ➢ L'idée qu'il **a avancée** est nulle. The idea he **put forward** is rubbish.
> ➢ Puis-je lui **avancer** une suggestion? Can I **put** a proposal **forward** to him?
> ➢ Nous **avons avancé** la même hypothèse l'année dernière. We **suggested** the same theory last year.
> ➢ Qu'**avancez**-vous exactement? What **are** you **suggesting** exactly?

4 - To make progress, to progress, to speed up

> ➢ Est-ce que ton anglais **avance**? Is your English **making progress/progressing**?
> ➢ Ça **avance** très lentement. It is **making** slow **progress**.
> ➢ Les réparations **ont** bien **avancé** n'est-ce pas? The repairs **have made** good **progress** haven't they?
> ➢ Le travail va **avancer** après la semaine prochaine. The work is going **to progress/to speed up** after next week.

5 - To lend (money), to give an advance

> ➢ Elle leur **a avancé** une grosse somme il y a quelques mois. She **lent** them a large amount of money a few months ago.

- ➢ Combien veux-tu lui **avancer**? How much do you want **to lend** him/her?
- ➢ J'ai demandé à mon patron de bien vouloir m'**avancer** une partie de mon salaire. I asked my boss whether he could **give** me **an advance** on my salary.
- ➢ Il ne veut rien lui **avancer**. He doesn't want **to give** him/her **an advance** of any amount.

6 - To commit oneself, to volunteer

- ➢ Je n'ai aucune intention de **m'avancer** pour quoi que ce soit. I have no intention whatsoever to **commit myself** for anything.
- ➢ Ils **s'avancent** sans vraiment comprendre la situation. They **commit themselves** without really understanding the situation.
- ➢ Dorénavant elle ne **s'avancera** plus. From now on she **will** never **volunteer** again.
- ➢ Personne n'a voulu **s'avancer**. Not a soul wanted **to volunteer**.

7 - To gain time (watches and clocks).

8 - To protrude, to jut out.

BÂILLER

1 - To yawn

- ➤ Arrête de **bâiller**. Stop **yawning**.
- ➤ Il faut mettre la main devant la bouche quand on **bâille**. You must put your hand in front of your mouth when you **yawn**.
- ➤ Je ne sais pas combien de fois j'**ai bâillé** aujourd'hui. I don't know how many times I **yawned** today.
- ➤ Elle **bâillait** toutes les cinq minutes. She **was yawning** every five minutes.

2 - To gape, to be ajar, to be loose/baggy

- ➤ Les coutures de ce vieux rideau **bâillent** partout maintenant. The seams of this old curtain **are gaping** everywhere now.
- ➤ Est-ce que la porte de la cuisine **a** toujours **bâillé** ainsi? **Has** the kitchen door always **been ajar** like this?
- ➤ Ses vieilles chaussures **bâillaient**. His/her old shoes **used to be loose/baggy**.
- ➤ L'encolure de ce chemisier **bâille** un peu trop pour mon goût. The neckline of this top **is** a little too **loose** for my taste.

BALANCER - SE BALANCER

1 - To swing

- ➤ Arrête de **balancer** les jambes. Stop **swinging** your legs.
- ➤ Le hamster **se balançait** à une branchette dans sa cage. The hamster **was swinging** from a small branch in his cage.
- ➤ Pourquoi est-ce que vous **balancez** vos sacs comme ça? Why do you **swing** your bags like this?
- ➤ Les enfants adorent **se balancer** sur ma vieille balançoire pendant des heures. The children enjoy **swinging** on my old swing for hours.

2 - To chuck, to kick out

- ➤ Qui **a balancé** ce stylo? Who **chucked** this pen?
- ➤ J'ai décidé de tout **balancer** à la poubelle. I decided **to chuck** everything into the dustbin.
- ➤ Il **a été balancé** de son poste la semaine dernière. He **has been kicked out** of his post last week.
- ➤ Tu vas te faire **balancer** du restaurant si tu continues. You are going to get **kicked out** of the restaurant if you carry on.

3 - To weigh up, to assess

➤ Une fois le pour et le contre **balancés** on s'aperçoit que ça revient au même. Once the for and against **has been weighed up** you realise that it makes no difference.

➤ Il va falloir bien tout **balancer** avant de prendre une décision. We shall have **to weigh up** everything carefully before deciding.

➤ Elle a l'intention de **balancer** les deux possibilités elle-même. She intends **to assess** the two possibilities herself.

➤ **Aviez**-vous **balancé** les avantages et les inconvénients? **Had** you **weighed up/assessed** the advantages and the drawbacks?

BONDIR

1 - To jump, to leap

➤ Tu m'as fait **bondir** de frayeur! You made me **jump** of fright!

➤ J'ai vu le lion **bondir** sur sa proie. I saw the lion **jump** on his prey.

> On **a** tous **bondi** de joie. We all **jumped** with joy.
> Il **a bondi** de sa chaise. He **leapt** from his chair.

2 - To dash, to rush

> Tout le monde **a bondi** hors du grand magasin.
> Everyone **dashed/rushed** out of the department store.
> Il nous faut **bondir** jusqu'à l'arrêt d'autobus sinon on va rater le bus. We need **to rush** to the bus stop or we are going to miss the bus.
> Le chien **a** tout de suite **bondi** dans la direction du bruit. The dog immediately **rushed** to where the noise was coming from.
> Ils **ont bondi** vers nous. They **rushed** towards us.

3 - To go mad, to be furious

> Ça nous a fait **bondir**. It made us **(go) mad**.
> Il **bondit** chaque fois que ça arrive. He **goes mad** every time that happens.
> Ils **ont bondi** comme prévu. They **were furious** as expected.
> Je suis sûre qu'elle **va bondir**. I do know that she is going **to be furious**.

BOUCLER - SE BOUCLER

1 - To close, to fasten, to lock

- ➢ Je n'arrive pas à **boucler** le sac il est trop plein. I can't **close** the bag it's too full.
- ➢ Regarde sa ceinture n'**est** pas **bouclée**. Look his/her belt **is** not **fastened**.
- ➢ Comment ça **se boucle** ce truc? How do you **close/fasten** this whatsit?
- ➢ **Bouclons** la porte et allons-y. Let's **lock** the door and go.

2 - To finish/complete/settle

- ➢ Voilà c'**est bouclé**. There we are it **is finished/is settled**.
- ➢ Ils **ont bouclé** les comptes pour l'année. They **have finished/have completed** the accounts for the year.
- ➢ Est-ce que l'affaire **est bouclée**? **Is** the matter **settled**?
- ➢ Cette question est loin d'**être bouclée**. This business is far from **being settled**.

3 - To curl (hair)

> Est-ce que vos cheveux **bouclent** naturellement? Is your hair naturally **curled**?
> Il essayait de **se boucler** les cheveux. He was trying **to curl** his hair.
> Elles **bouclaient** leurs cheveux pour le bal. They **used to curl** their hairs for the dance.
> Je vais me faire **boucler** les cheveux. I am going to have my hair **curled**.

4 - To shut away, to lock up

> Il le **bouclait** dans la cave. He **used to shut** him **away** in the cellar.
> Je **me bouclais** dans la salle de bains. I **used to shut myself away** in the bathroom.
> Les coupables **seront** sans doute **bouclés** dans les vingt-quatre heures. The culprits will probably **be locked up** within the next twenty-four hours.
> Elle les **a bouclés** dans la chambre. She **has locked** them **up** in the bedroom.

5 - To surround, to seal off, to cordon off (police).

BROUILLER - SE BROUILLER

1 - To blur, to make hazy

> ➤ La bruine **a brouillé** mes lunettes. The drizzle **has blurred** my spectacles.
> ➤ C'était dommage que la vue imprenable **était brouillée** par la brume. It was a pity that because of the mist the panoramic view **was hazy**.
> ➤ Le souvenir que j'ai de ces vacances **est** plutôt **brouillé** à présent. The recollection I have of that holiday **is** rather **blurred** these days.
> ➤ Avec l'âge la mémoire **se brouille**. One's memory becomes **blurred** with age.

2 - To mix, to muddle up, to confuse

> ➤ C'est toi qui **as brouillé** les coordonnées du client? Is it you who **mixed up** the customer's details?
> ➤ Elle **se brouille** facilement. She **gets muddled up** easily.
> ➤ Tout **était brouillé** dans sa tête. Everything **was muddled up** in his/her head.
> ➤ Toutes mes idées **se sont brouillées**. All my ideas **got confused**.

3 - To fall out

- ➤ Ils **se sont brouillés** il y a trois ans. They **fell out** (with each other) three years ago.
- ➤ Vous allez encore vous **brouiller** avec elle. You are going **to fall out** with her again.
- ➤ Je ne veux pas **me brouiller** avec ma famille. I don't want **to fall out** with my family.
- ➤ Malheureusement nous **nous sommes brouillés**. Sadly **we fell out** (with each other).

4 - To cloud over, to break (weather)

- ➤ Après dix heures le ciel **s'est brouillé**. After ten o'clock the sky **clouded over**.
- ➤ A partir de mardi le temps va **se brouiller**. The weather is going **to break up** after Tuesday.
- ➤ Chaque fois que je pars pour un week-end prolongé le temps **se brouille**. Every time I go away for a long weekend the weather **breaks up**.
- ➤ Vous pensez que le temps **se brouillera**? Do you think that the weather **will break up**?

5 - To jam, to cause interference (to the radio).

CAUSER

1 - To cause, to give

- ➢ Elle va **causer** des ennuis. She is going **to cause** trouble.
- ➢ On ne sait toujours pas ce qui **a causé** l'explosion. What **has caused** the explosion is still unknown.
- ➢ Ça risquerait de **causer** des malentendus. That would be likely **to cause** misunderstandings.
- ➢ Cela m'**avait causé** beaucoup de soucis. It **had caused/had given** me a lot of worries.

2 - To talk, to speak, to chat

- ➢ Elles **causent** chiffons depuis ce matin. They **have been talking** clothes since this morning.
- ➢ Il faudra que nous **causions**. We will have **to talk**.
- ➢ A qui **causes**-tu? Who **are** you **speaking** to?
- ➢ Ils **causaient** avec n'importe qui. They **used to chat** to anyone.

3 - To gossip

> On pourra **causer** tranquillement du matin au soir. We will be able **to gossip** to our hearts' content from morning to night.
> Je sais que les voisins **causent** sur moi. I know that the neighbours **gossip** about me.
> On **causait** sur lui dans le village. People **gossiped** about him in the village.
> Qu'ils **causent**! Let them **gossip**!

CÉDER

1 - To give up, to hand over

> Il **a** gentiment **cédé** sa place dans le métro à une dame enceinte. He kindly **gave up** his seat in the underground to a pregnant lady.
> Il est normal de **céder** la place aux personnes âgées. It is right **to give up** one's seat for old people.
> Pourriez-vous lui **céder** la parole une minute? Could you **hand** the conversation **over** to him/her for a minute?

➤ Nous avions décidé de **céder** notre mobile-home à notre fils. We had decided **to hand over** our mobile home to our son.

2 - To give way, to give in

➤ La glace **a cédé**. The ice **gave way**.
➤ Le petit pont pourrait **céder** sous le poids du camion. The small bridge could **give way** under the weight of the lorry.
➤ Elle **cède** trop souvent à ses enfants. She **gives way/gives in** to her children too often.
➤ Il est difficile de ne pas **céder** à cette tentation. It is hard not **to give way/give in** to this temptation.

3 - To sell, to dispose of, to let have

➤ Mes parents veulent **céder** leur commerce tout de suite après leur retraite. My parents want **to dispose of/to sell** their shop as soon as they retire.
➤ Tu ne vas pas **céder** tous tes biens voyons! Come on you can't **sell** all your possessions!
➤ Vous serait-il possible de nous **céder** une petite parcelle de votre pré par hasard? Would it be at all possible **to sell** us a small piece of your field?
➤ On **cède** le premier étage à nos enfants quand ils viennent. We **let** our children **have** the first floor when they visit.

CHARGER - SE CHARGER

1 - To load

- ➢ Il s'est fait mal en **chargeant** la voiture. He hurt himself whilst **loading** the car.
- ➢ Ils **chargeront** le camion ensemble. They **will load** the truck together.
- ➢ La vitrine de la pâtisserie **était chargée** de gâteaux délicieux. The shop window of the cake shop **was loaded** with delicious cakes.
- ➢ Qui **a chargé** l'appareil photo? Who **has loaded** the camera?

2 - To burden, to lumber, to trouble

- ➢ Nous **étions chargés** d'impôts. We **were burdened** with taxes.
- ➢ Pourquoi **nous charger** de leurs problèmes? Why **be burdened/be lumbered** with their problems?
- ➢ Ils m'**avaient chargé** de faire la vaisselle tout le mois. They **had lumbered** me with the washing up for the whole month.
- ➢ Ce n'est pas la peine de **vous charger** la mémoire avec ces faits. It is useless **to trouble** your head with this information.

3 - To take care, to put in charge

- ➤ Elle va **se charger** des commissions. She is going **to take care** of the shopping.
- ➤ Qui **est chargé** du ménage ici? Who **takes care/is in charge** of the housework here?
- ➤ Je ne veux pas **être chargé** des boissons. I don't want **to be put in charge** of the drinks.
- ➤ Ils m'**ont chargé** de leurs chats. They **put** me **in charge** of their cats.

4 - To charge, to attack

- ➤ Le sanglier pourrait **charger** d'un coup. The boar could suddenly **charge**.
- ➤ Il n'est pas surprenant que la pauvre bête s'est mise à **charger** la foule. It is not surprising that the poor animal started **to charge/to attack** the crowd.
- ➤ Allez-y **chargez**! Go on **charge**!
- ➤ Nos supérieurs nous avaient ordonnés de **charger**. Our superiors had ordered us **to charge**.

5 - To charge (someone with a crime).

COMBLER

1 - To fill up/in

- ➢ Comment va-t-on **combler** toutes ces fentes? How are we going **to fill up** all these cracks?
- ➢ Son absence va laisser un vide impossible à **combler**. His/her departure is going to leave a void impossible **to fill**.
- ➢ Vous **avez comblé** le trou avec quoi? What **did** you **fill** the hole with?
- ➢ Il te faudrait **combler** des lacunes dans tes connaissances générales. You really should **fill in** some gaps in your general knowledge.

2 - To overwhelm, to fulfil

- ➢ La gentillesse de tout le monde nous **a** vraiment **comblés**. The thoughtfulness shown by everybody did **overwhelm** us.
- ➢ Je pense que cela les **comblerait**. I think that it **would overwhelm/would fulfil** them.
- ➢ Elle **comble** tous mes rêves. She **fulfils** all my dreams.
- ➢ Lorsque je suis en famille je **suis comblé**. When I am at home with my family I **am fulfilled**.

3 - To shower with

> Il ne veut pas que vous le **combliez** de faveurs. He doesn't want you **to shower** him with favours.
> Les gosses **ont été comblés** de jouets pour Noël comme toujours. As always the kids **were showered** with toys at Christmas.
> Elle **comble** ses petits-enfants de louanges. She **showers** her grandchildren with praise.
> Je veux la **combler** de cadeaux cette année. I want **to shower** her with presents this year.

COMMANDER - SE COMMANDER

1 - To order

> Qu'est-ce que tu **as commandé**? What **have** you **ordered**?
> Voilà trois semaines que j'**ai commandé** des meubles. I **ordered** some furniture three weeks ago.
> Quand **avaient**-ils **commandé** les fleurs? When **had** they **ordered** the flowers?
> Il nous faut **commander** du charbon. We need **to order** some coal.

2 - To commission

> Il lui **a commandé** un portrait de sa femme. He **commissioned** a portrait of his wife from him/her.
> Cet artiste aime qu'on lui **commande** son travail au moins un an à l'avance. This artist likes his work **to be commissioned** at least a year in advance.
> Ça **avait été commandé**? **Had** it **been commissioned**?
> Le conseil municipal ne savait pas qui **commander** pour cette oeuvre. The council did not know who **to commission** for this work.

3 - To be in charge, to boss about

> Tu veux toujours **commander**. You always want **to be in charge**.
> Qui **commandait** chez toi? Who **used to be in charge** in your house?
> C'est eux qui **commanderont**. They **will be in charge**.
> Arrêtez de nous **commander**! Stop **bossing** us **about**!

4 - To control

> Elle n'a jamais su les **commander**. She could never **control** them.

➤ La vitesse des essuie-glaces **se commande** comme ceci. The speed of the windscreen wipers **is controlled** like this.

➤ Il n'arrive plus à **commander** sa main droite. He can't **control** his right hand anymore.

➤ Essayez donc de **commander** vos émotions. Do try **to control** your emotions.

5 - To command, to compel

➤ Elle **a** toujours **commandé** tout le respect de ses collègues. She **has** always **commanded** great respect from her colleagues.

➤ C'est une action qui **commande** l'admiration de tous. This is an action that **commands** everyone's approval.

➤ Ça **commande** la prudence. That **compels** one to be cautious.

➤ Cet exemple ne peut **commander** qu'une grande réflexion. This example can only **compel** one to think very carefully indeed.

COMPOSER - SE COMPOSER

1 - To make up, to form

- ➤ Où peut-on trouver les ingrédients qui **composent** cette recette? Where can one find all the ingredients that **make up** this recipe?
- ➤ Les émissions de réalité télévision semblent toujours **être composées** d'un mélange de personnalités. Reality television shows always seem **to be made up** of people of mixed personalities.
- ➤ Qui sera responsable de **composer** le menu végétarien? Who will be responsible for **making up** a vegetarian menu?
- ➤ Cela **composerait** un tout? Would that **form** a whole?

2 - To compose, to do, to arrange

- ➤ Cette lettre **est** plutôt mal **composée**. This letter **is** somewhat poorly **composed/done**.
- ➤ Il va **composer** un poème pour sa mère. He is going **to compose** a poem for his mother.
- ➤ Qui **a composé** les plates bandes? Who **has done** the flowerbeds?
- ➤ Elle **est** vraiment bien **composée** cette vitrine. This shop window **is** really well **arranged**.

3 - To consist, to comprise

> De quoi **se compose** ce produit exactement? What **does** this product **consist** of exactly?

> Le jouet **se composait** de trois parties. The toy **consisted** of three parts.

> C'est un plat **composé** de différents féculents. This dish **consists** of different pulses.

> Cette machine **se compose** de plusieurs pièces japonaises. This machine **comprises** several Japanese parts.

4 - To dial, to enter

> Il suffit de **composer** le numéro vert suivant. All you need do is **dial** the following free telephone number.

> J'avais oublié de **composer** l'indicatif. I had forgotten **to dial** the dialling code.

> Il faut **composer** son code personnel à la place d'une signature. You must **enter** your personal code instead of signing.

> Si vous voulez bien **composer** votre code personnel ici maintenant. If you wouldn't mind **entering** your personal code here now.

5 - To sit, to take (a test, an exam).

COMPRENDRE - SE COMPRENDRE

1 - To understand

- ➤ Nous **nous sommes compris**. We **understood each other**.
- ➤ Est-ce que vous **comprenez** l'allemand? Do you **understand** German?
- ➤ Il n'**avait** rien **compris** du tout. He **had** not **understood** anything at all.
- ➤ C'est quelque chose que je ne **comprendrai** jamais. That is something that I **will** never **understand**.

2 - To realize

- ➤ Je n'**avais** pas **compris**. I **had** not **realized**.
- ➤ Elle **a compris** qu'il voulait la quitter. She **realized** that he wanted to leave her.
- ➤ C'est alors que nous **avons compris**. That's when we **realized**.
- ➤ Ils ont mis longtemps à **comprendre**. It took them a long time **to realize**.

3 - To be composed of, to consist of, to be made with

- ➤ Le livre **comprend** dix chapitres. The book **is composed of** ten chapters.
- ➤ Votre ville **comprend** combien d'arrondissements? Your town **is composed of** how many arrondissements?
- ➤ Ça **comprend** plusieurs parties. It **consists of** several parts.
- ➤ Ce plat **comprend** beaucoup de crème. This dish **is made with** a lot of cream

4 - To include, to be fitted with

- ➤ La ferme à vendre **comprenait** trois petits hangars. The farm for sale **included** three small outbuildings.
- ➤ Est-ce que le petit-déjeuner **sera compris**? Will breakfast **be included**?
- ➤ Les frais de déplacement n'**ont** pas **été compris**. Travelling expenses **have** not **been included**.
- ➤ Mon nouveau lave-linge **comprend** l'option sèche-linge. My new washing machine **is fitted with** a tumble drying function.

COMPTER

1 - To count

- ➢ Il sait déjà **compter** jusqu'à vingt. He can already **count** up to twenty.
- ➢ **As**-tu **compté** les places? **Did** you **count** the seats?
- ➢ Nous allons **compter** les jours. We are going **to count** the days.
- ➢ Il ne reste plus qu'a **compter** l'argent. All there is left to do is **count** the money.

2 - To matter, to count

- ➢ Ce n'est pas ce qui **compte** maintenant. This is not what **matters** now.
- ➢ Qu'est-ce qui **comptait** le plus à votre avis? What **mattered** the most in your opinion?
- ➢ J'ai l'impression de ne plus **compter**. I feel as though I don't **count** anymore.
- ➢ Ce qui **compte** c'est son devoir. What **matters/counts** is one's responsibility.

3 - To rely, to count

> ➢ Nous voulons absolument **compter** sur toi. We want **to rely/to count** on you completely.
> ➢ Tu peux **compter** sur nous. You can **rely/count** on us.
> ➢ Nous **avions compté** sur eux à tort. It had been a mistake **to rely** on them.
> ➢ On n'a jamais pu **compter** sur lui. You could never **rely/count** on him.

4 - To allow, to reckon

> ➢ Il faut **compter** quatre semaines pour la livraison. You have **to allow** four weeks for delivery.
> ➢ Nous **avons compté** que dix-huit personnes viendront. We **reckon** that eighteen people will come.
> ➢ Combien **avait**-il **compté** pour la réparation? How much **had** he **reckoned** the repair would cost?
> ➢ J'**avais compté** qu'une baguette suffirait pour trois enfants. I **had reckoned** that one baguette would be enough for three children.

5 - To include, to take into account

> ➢ Est-ce que tu m'**as compté**? **Did** you **include** me?
> ➢ Avez-vous oublié de **compter** les coups de téléphone? Did you forget **to include** the telephone calls?

- ➤ Elle n'**avait** pas **compté** ça. She **had** not **taken** that into account.
- ➤ Il faut aussi **compter** tout ça. You also have **to take** all that **into account**.

6 - To charge

- ➤ Il leur **a compté** 25 € par heure pour refaire la cuisine. He **charged** them 25 € an hour to redecorate the kitchen.
- ➤ Le garage pour votre voiture **sera compté** sur la note. The car park for your car **will be charged** on the invoice.
- ➤ Vous avez oublié de **compter** les apéritifs sur l'addition. You forgot **to charge** for the aperitifs on the bill.
- ➤ Vous lui **avez compté** combien pour le travail? How much **did** you **charge** him/her for the work?

7 - To have

- ➤ Le village ne **compte** que cent cinquante habitants. The village only **has** one hundred and fifty inhabitants.
- ➤ Ma fille **compte** trois Françaises parmi ses meilleurs amis. My daughter **has** three French girls amongst her best friends.
- ➤ Leur ville **compte** plusieurs ponts pittoresques. Their town **has** a number of picturesque bridges.

➢ C'est la région qui **compte** le plus de châteaux. This is the area that **has** the highest number of castles.

8 - To intend to, to plan

➢ Quand **comptes**-tu venir? When **do** you **intend** to come?
➢ C'est ce qu'ils **comptaient** faire. That is what they **intended** to do.
➢ Nous **comptons** déménager avant la fin de l'année. We **plan** to move house before the end of the year.
➢ Je **compte** arriver avant dix heures. I **intend/plan** to arrive before ten.

9 - To rank.

CONFONDRE - SE CONFONDRE

1 - To mix up, to confuse, to mistake

➤ **Avez**-vous **confondu** les dates? **Did** you **mix up** the dates?

➤ Elle **a confondu** ton anniversaire avec celui de ta sœur. She **confused** your birthday with your sister's birthday.

➤ Ne **confondez** pas ces deux choses. Don't **confuse** these two things.

➤ Nous vous **avons confondu** avec quelqu'un d'autre. We **have mistaken** you for someone else.

2 - To astound, to confound, to amaze, to overwhelm

➤ Leur nouvelle les **a** complètement **confondus**. Their news completely **astounded/confounded/amazed** them.

➤ Ils **seront** sans doute **confondus**. They **will** most probably **be amazed**.

➤ Notre visite surprise pourrait la **confondre**. Our surprise visit could **overwhelm** her.

➤ Ce témoignage de son amitié m'**a** vraiment **confondu**. This proof of his/her friendship **has** really **overwhelmed** me.

3 - To meet up, to merge

➤ La mer et le ciel **se confondent** à l'horizon. The sky and the sea **merge in the distance.**

➤ Emmène-moi où les deux ruisseaux **se confondent**. Take me where the two streams **meet up**.

➤ Regarde la forme amusante de nos ombres qui **se confondent**. Look at the funny shape of our shadows as they **merge**.

➤ Tous ces souvenirs **se sont** complètement **confondus** dans ma tête. All these souvenirs merged together in my head.

CONVENIR

1 - To be advisable, to be proper, to be right, to be appropriate

> ➤ Penses-tu qu'il **conviendrait** de leur écrire? Do you think that **it would be advisable** to write to them?
> ➤ Cela ne **convient** pas du tout dans les circonstances actuelles. This **is** not at all **right** in the present circumstances.
> ➤ Il **aurait convenu** de téléphoner. It **would have been advisable/appropriate** to phone.
> ➤ Que **convient**-il de faire maintenant? What **is** the **appropriate/proper** thing to do now?

2 - To admit, to acknowledge, to accept

> ➤ Ils **ont convenu** de leur erreur de mal gré. They reluctantly **admitted** to their mistake.
> ➤ Vous **convenez** de votre paresse? **Do** you **admit** that you are lazy?
> ➤ Ils ne **conviendront** jamais qu'ils se sentent supérieurs aux autres. They will never **admit** that they feel superior to others.
> ➤ Elle **a** enfin **convenu** que j'avais eu raison. She finally **admitted/acknowledged/accepted** that I had been right.

3 - To suit, to be suitable, to be convenient

> Est-ce que neuf heures vous **convient**? **Would** nine o'clock **suit** you?
> Est-ce que ces arrangements leur **conviendraient**? **Would** these arrangements **suit** them?
> Le climat espagnol ne **convient** pas à tout le monde. Spanish weather doesn't **suit** everybody.
> Mardi me **convient** cette semaine. Tuesday is convenient for me this week.

4 - To agree, to accept, to arrange

> Nous **avons convenu** de les rencontrer samedi prochain. We **agreed/accepted/arranged** to meet them next Saturday.
> Elle a téléphoné hier soir comme **convenu**. She phoned last evening as **agreed/arranged**.
> Qu'est-ce qui **a été convenu** à la fin? What **was agreed/was arranged** in the end?
> Ils **ont convenu** de se voir? **Did** they **agree** to see/meet each other?

CRAQUER

1 - To creak, to squeak, to crackle, to crunch

- ➤ Elle avait entendu quelque chose **craquer**. She had heard something **creak/squeak/crackle/crunch**.
- ➤ Tu entends le parquet **craquer**? Can you hear the floor **creaking**?
- ➤ Le feu **craque** plus que d'habitude ce soir. The fire **crackles** more than usual tonight.
- ➤ Les feuilles mortes **craquaient** sous nos pas. The dead leaves **crunched** under our steps.

2 - To crack, to break, to rip, to split

- ➤ La glace a fini par **craquer** sous le poids. The ice **cracked** under the weight in the end.
- ➤ La glissière de ton pantalon **a craqué**. Your trousers' zip **has broken**.
- ➤ Attention ça va **craquer**! Careful it is going **to break/to rip/to split**.
- ➤ Quelques branches **ont craqué** dans le vent. A few branches **broke** in the wind.

3 - To fall apart, to collapse

> ➢ Elle **avait craqué** sous la pression. She **had fallen apart** under the pressure.
> ➢ Plusieurs personnes **ont craqué** pendant le marathon. Several people **collapsed** during the marathon.
> ➢ Tu vas **craquer** si ça continue. You are going **to fall apart/to collapse** if this goes on.
> ➢ Quand il a appris la nouvelle il **a craqué**. When he heard the news **he fell apart/collapsed**.

4 - To give in, to give way, to be unable to resist

> ➢ Ce n'est pas le moment de **craquer** voyons! Come on this is no time for **giving in**.
> ➢ Les enfants pensent qu'elle **craquera** tôt ou tard. The children believe that sooner or later she **will give in/will give way**.
> ➢ Quand j'ai vu cette robe de plage j'**ai craqué**, je l'ai achetée. When I saw that beach dress I **couldn't resist** buying it.
> ➢ Tant pis pour le régime je **craque** je prends un troisième croissant. Never mind the diet I **can't resist** a third croissant.

DÉBOUCHER - SE DÉBOUCHER

1 - To uncork, to open, to take the top off

- ➤ Quand allez-vous **déboucher** le vin? When are you going **to uncork/to open/to take the top off** the wine?
- ➤ Ce n'est pas facile à **déboucher** ce type de bouteille. This type of bottle is not easy **to open**.
- ➤ Ne laisse pas ça **débouché** ça risque de s'évaporer. Don't leave that **open/with the top off** it might evaporate.
- ➤ Qui **a débouché** ma bouteille de parfum? Who **has taken off the top** of my bottle of perfume?

2 - To unblock

- ➤ Il a pu **déboucher** la gouttière. He has managed **to unblock** the gutter.
- ➤ Ça **s'est débouché** tout seul. It **unblocked** itself.
- ➤ Ils n'**ont** pas encore **débouché** l'évier. They **have** not **unblocked** the sink yet.
- ➤ Je vais essayer de **déboucher** ce tuyau. I am going to try and **unblock** this pipe.

3 - To emerge, to come out

- ➢ Tout à coup un camion **a débouché** du virage. From the bend a lorry suddenly **emerged**.
- ➢ J'aime regarder les trains **déboucher** du tunnel. I love watching the trains **come out** of the tunnel.
- ➢ C'était minuit quand j'ai vu quatre ou cinq garçons **déboucher** du coin de la rue. It was midnight when I saw four or five boys **emerge** from the corner of the street.
- ➢ Soudain une moto de CRS **a débouché** des ténèbres. All of a sudden a motorbike from the State security police **came out** of the dark.

4 - To lead

- ➢ Cette ruelle **débouche** sur la place principale. This path **leads** to the main square.
- ➢ Cela n'**avait** pas **débouché** où nous avions cru que ça **déboucherait**. It did not **lead** where we had thought it **would lead**.
- ➢ Sur quoi est-ce que toutes ces préparations vont **déboucher**? All these preparations are going **to lead** to what?
- ➢ A son avis cela ne **débouchera** sur rien. In his/her opinion it **will lead** nowhere.

DÉBROUILLER - SE DÉBROUILLER

1 - To untangle, to unravel, to disentangle, to sort out

> ➢ Est-ce qu'elle pourrait **débrouiller** cette laine? Could she **untangle** this wool?
> ➢ Le pêcheur est en train de **débrouiller** sa ligne. The fisherman is in the middle of **unravelling/disentangling** his fishing line.
> ➢ Je me demande si un jour on pourra **débrouiller** ce mystère. I wonder whether we will ever be able **to unravel** this mystery.
> ➢ Vous devez **débrouiller** ce problème au plus tôt. You must **sort out** the problem as soon as possible.

2 - To manage, to cope

> ➢ Tu **t'es débrouillé** de le faire à temps? **Did** you **manage** to do it in time?
> ➢ Ils **se sont** très bien **débrouillés**. They **managed/coped** very well.
> ➢ Comment **vous êtes**-vous **débrouillé** pour les convaincre? How **did** you **manage** to convince them?
> ➢ Il va falloir **nous débrouiller** d'une façon ou d'une autre. We will have **to manage/to cope** one way or another.

DÉCHARGER - SE DÉCHARGER

1 - To unload

> Je regarde les employés de l'aéroport **décharger** les valises de l'avion. I am watching the workers at the airport **unloading** the cases from the plane.
> Est-ce que vous **avez** déjà **déchargé** la voiture? **Have** you already **unloaded** the car?
> Pourrait-il **décharger** la camionnette derrière le magasin? Could he **unload** the lorry behind the shop?
> Il vaut mieux **décharger** les armes maintenant. It is best **to unload** the guns now.

2 - To unburden, to relieve, to vent

> Elle a décidé de **décharger** sa conscience une fois pour toutes. She decided to **unburden** her conscience once and for all.
> Merci encore de votre aide vous nous **avez déchargés** d'une sale corvée. Thank you once more for your help you **did relieve** us from a dreadful chore.
> Il **a** toujours **déchargé** sa colère sur eux. He **has** always **vented** his anger on them.
> Il est nécessaire que tu **te décharges** de ces frustrations. You must **vent** these frustrations.

3 - To release, to discharge, to exempt, to relieve

- ➢ Quand pensez-vous qu'il **sera déchargé**? When do you think that he **will be released/will be discharged**?
- ➢ Elle est contente d'**avoir été déchargée** de ce travail. She is pleased that she **has been exempted** from that job.
- ➢ **Seront**-ils **déchargés** de ces frais? **Will** they **be exempted** from these expenses?
- ➢ Je viens d'être **déchargé** de mes anciennes responsabilités. I have just been **relieved** from my former duties.

DÉCOLLER - SE DÉCOLLER

1 - To unstick

- ➢ Les enveloppes **se sont** toutes **décollées**. All the envelopes **have become unstuck**.
- ➢ Quand va-t-il **décoller** tout ça? When is he going **to unstick** all this?
- ➢ Nous **décollerons** toutes les affiches demain. We **will unstick** all the posters tomorrow.
- ➢ Je veux **décoller** le timbre pour ma collection. I want **to unstick** the stamp for my collection.

2 - To get rid (of people)

- ➢ Pas moyen de **me décoller** d'elle. I simply could not **get rid** of her.
- ➢ Tu aurais pu essayer de me **décoller** d'eux. You could have tried **to get rid** of them for me.
- ➢ Il est toujours difficile de **se décoller** de ces gens. It is always a problem **getting rid** of these people.
- ➢ Vous **vous êtes décollé** de lui à quelle heure? You **got rid** of him at what time?

3 - To take off, to lift off

- ➢ Tous les avions vont **décoller** en retard ce matin. All the planes are going **to take off** late this morning.
- ➢ La fusée doit **décoller** à six heures. The rocket is due **to lift off** at six o'clock.
- ➢ Est-ce que son affaire a fini par **décoller**? Did his/her business **take off** in the end?
- ➢ Espérons que la compagnie **décollera** comme prévu. Let's hope that the company **will take off** as envisaged.

DÉCOUVRIR - SE DÉCOUVRIR

1 - To discover, to find out

➢ Qu'**ont**-ils **découvert**? What **did** they **discover**?

➢ Je crois que j'**ai découvert** leur secret. I believe that I **have discovered** their secret.

➢ Elles **ont découvert** qu'il avait une aptitude pour l'anglais. They **discovered** that he had a gift for English.

➢ Qu'est-ce que vous espérez **découvrir**? What do you hope **to find out**?

2 - To uncover, to take off (covers)

➢ Je l'ai trouvé tout **découvert** dans son lit. I found him all **uncovered** in his bed.

➢ Il vaut mieux ne pas **découvrir** la casserole pendant la cuisson. It is better not **to take** the lid **off** the saucepan whilst it is cooking.

➢ Ne te **découvre** pas ce n'est que le mois d'avril. Don't **take** anything **off** it's only April.

➢ Nous **avions découvert** tous les plats. We **had taken off** all the tops off the dishes.

3 - To reveal

> - Il est souhaitable de **découvrir** son cœur de temps en temps. It is a good thing **to reveal** one's emotions from time to time.
> - Elle ne **se découvrira** jamais à personne. She **will** never **reveal** herself to anyone.
> - Vous regrettez de **vous être découvert** à vos voisins? Do you regret **revealing yourself** to your neighbours?
> - Ton décolleté **découvre** presque tout! Your neckline **reveals** nearly everything.

4 - To clear (weather): reflexive form.

DÉFENDRE - SE DÉFENDRE

1 - To defend, to protect

> - Nous les **défendrons**. We **will defend** them.
> - Ils **se sont défendus** courageusement. They bravely **defended themselves**.
> - Qui pourra vous **défendre**? Who will be able **to defend/to protect** you?
> - Elle **défendait** toujours les animaux. She always **used to protect** animals.

2 - To forbid

> Il **est défendu** de marcher sur les pelouses. It **is forbidden** to walk on the grass.
> Elle nous **a défendus** de fumer. She **forbade** us to smoke.
> Pourquoi leur **avez**-vous **défendu** de venir? Why **did you forbid** them to come?
> C'est quelque chose que nous **nous sommes** toujours **défendus**. This is something that we **have** always **forbidden ourselves** (to do).

3 - To deny

> Je **me suis défendu** jusqu'au bout. I **denied** it to the end.
> Pour quelle raison ne **se défend**-il pas? Why doesn't he **deny** it?
> Nous n'avons pas pu **nous défendre**. We couldn't **deny** it.
> Ils ne **s'étaient** pas **défendus**. They **had** not **denied** it.

4 - To refrain (from).

DÉGAGER - SE DÉGAGER

1 - To free, to rescue, to disentangle

- ➢ Vous voilà **dégagé** de cette obligation. You **are** now **free** from that commitment.
- ➢ Le passage devra rester **dégagé**. The opening will have to be kept **free**.
- ➢ Les pompiers sont en train de **dégager** les blessés des débris. The firemen **are rescuing/are freeing** the injured people from the wreckage.
- ➢ On a mis trois heures à **dégager** cette vieille malle des buissons dans le jardin. It took us three hours **to disentangle** this old trunk from the bushes in the garden.

2 - To clear

- ➢ Le ciel **s'est** un peu **dégagé**. The sky **cleared** a little.
- ➢ La police **a dégagé** le parking des manifestants. The police **cleared** the demonstrators off the car park.
- ➢ Je voudrais que mon nez **se dégage** avant l'entrevue. I would hope that my nose **would clear up** before the interview.
- ➢ Voulez-vous **dégager** le couloir des valises? Would you mind **clearing** the corridor of the suitcases?

3 - To give off, to come out, to radiate

> ➤ Les radiateurs ne **dégagent** plus assez de chaleur. The radiators don't **give off** enough heat any more.
> ➤ Il y a de la fumée qui **se dégage** de la fenêtre. There is some smoke **coming out** of the window.
> ➤ Une odeur de moisi **se dégage** de cette pièce. A mouldy smell **comes out** of this room.
> ➤ Il **dégage** un goût de vivre unique. He **radiates** a unique gift for life.

4 - To bring out, to draw (a conclusion, an idea).

DÉROULER - SE DÉROULER

1 - To unwind, to unroll

> ➤ Sa petite-fille **a déroulé** toute la bobine. His/her granddaughter **unwound** the whole bobbin.
> ➤ Pouvez-vous **dérouler** le tuyau d'arrosage? Can you **unwind** the hose?
> ➤ Est-ce que quelqu'un peut m'aider à **dérouler** le tapis? Can somebody help me **unroll** the carpet?

> On va **dérouler** le vieux document avec grande précaution. We are going **to unroll** this old document very carefully indeed.

2 - To take place, to unfold

> Normalement la fête **se déroule** le premier mai. Usually the fête **takes place** on the first of May.
> Quand est-ce que cet évènement doit **se dérouler**? When is this event due **to take place**?
> Ça **se déroulait** toujours devant la gare. It always used **to take place** outside the station.
> J'ai vu ma vie **se dérouler** dans ma tête. I saw my life **unfold** in my head.

3 - To progress, to develop

> Je me demande comment va **se dérouler** la réunion. I am wondering how the meeting will **progress**.
> J'espère que ça **se déroulera** aussi bien que possible. I hope that it **will progress** in the best possible way.
> Impossible de savoir comment cette histoire **se déroulera**. There is no way of knowing how this affair **will develop**.
> Tout **s'est** très bien **déroulé**. Everything **developed** satisfactorily.

DESCENDRE

1 - To go down, to come down, to walk down

> ➢ Vous **êtes descendu** trop tôt. You **went down** too early.
> ➢ Nous **descendrons** pour notre petit-déjeuner vers sept heures. We **will come down** for our breakfast around seven.
> ➢ Demandez-lui de **descendre**. Ask him **to come down**.
> ➢ Ils **descendaient** la rue principale ensemble. They **were walking down** the main street together.

2 - To take down, to bring down, to carry down

> ➢ Il était en train de **descendre** l'échelle dans la cave. He was **taking** the ladder **down** to the cellar.
> ➢ Que faut-il **descendre**? What do I need **to bring down**?
> ➢ Elle m'a descendu mes pantoufles. She **brought** my sleepers **down** for me.
> ➢ Tu pourrais **descendre** le plateau? Could you **carry** the tray **down**?

3 - To get off/out of (any means of transport)

- ➢ On va bientôt **descendre** du train. We are going **to get off** the train soon.
- ➢ Quand je l'ai vu il **descendait** de la voiture. When I saw him he **was getting out** of the car.
- ➢ Tous les passagers **étaient** déjà **descendus** de l'avion. All the passengers **had** already **got off** the plane.
- ➢ Où voulez-vous **descendre**? Where do you want **to get off**?

4 - To lower, to drop

- ➢ Il voudrait qu'on **descende** toutes les étagères dans cette pièce. He would rather we **lowered** all the shelves in this room.
- ➢ On pourrait **descendre** le tableau de quelques centimètres. We could **lower** the picture down a few centimetres.
- ➢ Ce sera mieux quand ils auront descendu le miroir. It will be better once they **have dropped** the mirror a little.
- ➢ **Descends** les bras. **Lower/drop** your arms.

5 - To take after, to be descended from

- ➢ Tu **descends** bien de ton père. You do **take after** your father.

> ➢ Mais de qui **il descend** lui? Who **does** he **take after**?
> ➢ Elle **descendait** d'une famille artistique. She **descended** from an artistic family.
> ➢ Vous **descendez** tous de cette famille? **Do** you all **descend** from this family?

6 - To kill, to shoot down

> ➢ Il est clair que quelqu'un voulait le **descendre**. It is obvious that someone wanted **to kill** him.
> ➢ Un homme **a descendu** sa femme après une dispute. A man **killed** his wife after a row.
> ➢ Il a dit qu'il les **descendrait** un jour. He said that one day he **would kill** them.
> ➢ C'est le deuxième hélicoptère qui **a été descendu**. This is the second helicopter that **has been shot down**.

7 - To stay (in hotels).

8 - To descend on, to land at (people's places).

9 - To raid (police).

DEVOIR - SE DEVOIR

1 - To owe

- ➤ Je lui **devais** beaucoup d'argent. I **owed** him/her a lot of money.
- ➤ Il ne nous **doit** aucune explication. He doesn't **owe** us an explanation whatsoever.
- ➤ Nous vous **devons** un grand service. We **owe** you a big favour.
- ➤ Vous lui **deviez** des excuses. You **owed** him/her an apology.

2 - To be one's duty

- ➤ Nous **devons** tous nous occuper de nos vieux parents. It **is our duty** to look after our old parents.
- ➤ Tout le monde **doit** aider quelqu'un en danger. It **is the duty** of everyone to help a person in danger.
- ➤ Vous **vous deviez** de donner l'exemple. It **was your duty** to give an example.
- ➤ Ils **se devaient** d'être ponctuels. It **was their duty** to be punctual.

3 - To have to, must

- ➤ Vous **devez** travailler le samedi? **Do** you **have** to work on Saturdays?
- ➤ Ils **ont dû** leur obéir. They **had** to obey them.
- ➤ On **devra** arriver avant six heures. We **will have** to arrive before six.
- ➤ Elles **doivent** quitter la ville le 15 juillet. They **must** leave the town on the 15th of July.

4 - To be due (to do), to be supposed (to do)

- ➤ Elle **devait** téléphoner dimanche. She **was due** to phone on Sunday.
- ➤ Quand est-ce que tu **dois** aller chez le dentiste? When **are** you **due** to go to the dentist's?
- ➤ Franchement je ne sais pas ce que je **dois** faire. Honestly I don't know what I **am supposed** to do.
- ➤ Le taxi **aurait dû** être là il y a vingt minutes. The taxi **was supposed** to be here twenty minutes ago.

5 - To be bound (to do), must

- ➤ Ils **doivent** tout savoir maintenant. They **are bound** to know everything now.
- ➤ Ça **devait** arriver un jour ou l'autre. It **was bound** to happen one of these days.

> ➤ Ce **doit** être trop tard à présent. **It must** be too late now.
> ➤ Vous **devez** être fiers de votre frère. You **must** be proud of your brother.

DIRE - SE DIRE

1 - To say

> ➤ Qu'est-ce que **dit** la loi? What **does** the law **say**?
> ➤ Elle ne sait pas ce qu'ils **diront**. She doesn't know what they **will say**.
> ➤ Il **disait** toujours la même chose. He always **used to say** the same thing.
> ➤ Si j'étais toi je ne **dirais** rien. If I were you I **would** not **say** anything.

2 - To tell

> ➤ Nous aurions dû vous le **dire** plus tôt. We should have **told** you earlier.
> ➤ Ne le **dis** à personne. Don't **tell** anyone.
> ➤ Je vais tout leur **dire**. I am going **to tell** them everything.
> ➤ Qu'est-ce que vous lui **avez dit**? What **did** you **tell** him/her?

3 - To think

> **Dire** que ça aurait pu être moi. **To think** that it could have been me.
> C'est ce qu'ils **se sont dit**. That's what they **thought**.
> On **dirait** qu'il l'avait fait exprès. You **would think** that he did it on purpose.
> Que **dis**-tu d'un week-end à Nice? What **do** you **think** about a weekend in Nice?

4 - To feel like (something), to fancy

> Ça ne me **dit** rien aujourd'hui d'aller au cinéma. I don't **feel like** going to the cinema today.
> Ça ne leur **dit** pas grand chose. They don't **feel like** it/**fancy** it very much.
> Est-ce que ça vous **dirait** d'emprunter nos vélos? **Do** you **feel like**/**fancy** borrowing our bicycles?
> Qu'est-ce qui vous **dit**? What **do** you **fancy**?

5 - To claim to be

> Il **se dit** licencié ès lettres. He **claims to be** a graduate in Arts.
> Elle **se dit** à moitié française. She **claims to be** half French.
> Ils **se disaient** les plus riches de la rue. They **used to claim to be** the most wealthy people in the street.
> Il **s'est** encore **dit** malade. He **claimed to be** ill again.

DIRIGER - SE DIRIGER

1 - To run, to manage, to be in charge, to lead

- ➤ Qui pourrait **diriger** l'usine pendant son absence? Who could **run** the factory when he/she is away?
- ➤ Il **dirigeait** l'entreprise depuis quatre ans. He **had been managing** the firm for four years.
- ➤ Elle n'a jamais su **diriger** ses finances. She has never been able **to manage** her finances.
- ➤ Je **dirigerai** une équipe de six personnes. I **will be in charge of/will lead** a team of six people.

2 - To control, to conduct

- ➤ Tu as toujours aimé **diriger** les autres. You have always enjoyed **controlling** others.
- ➤ Ce n'est pas la monarchie qui **dirige** le pays. It is not the monarchy that **controls** the country.
- ➤ Je voudrais **diriger** cet entretien. I would like **to control/to conduct** this interview.
- ➤ Leur ami aimerait **diriger** un orchestre. Their friend would love **to conduct** an orchestra.

3 - To turn, to direct, to steer

> Elle **a dirigé** son regard vers nous. She **turned** her look towards us.
> Ils essaient de **diriger** leur fils vers la médecine. They are trying **to direct** their son towards medicine.
> Pourriez-vous nous **diriger** dans la direction du zoo? Could you **direct** us towards the zoo?
> J'ai vu une voiture blanche **se diriger** dangereusement vers la gauche. I saw a white car **steering** in a dangerous way towards the left.

4 - To send, to direct

> Je les **ai dirigés** vers vous. I **sent** them to you.
> Où dois-je **diriger** leur courrier? Where must I **send** their post?
> Nous **dirigerons** les touristes au restaurant pour midi. We **will direct** the tourists to the restaurant at lunchtime.
> Il faut **diriger** tout ça à la nouvelle adresse. You have **to send/to direct** all that to the new address.

5 - To point, to direct, to aim

> Arrête de **diriger** ton couteau sur moi et coupe le pain. You stop **pointing** your knife at me and cut the bread.

> ➤ Tu peux **diriger** la lampe sur la gauche? Can you **point/direct/aim** the light towards the left?
> ➤ Je suis sûr que cette réflexion **était dirigée** sur moi. I am certain that this observation **was directed/was aimed** at me.
> ➤ Ces insultes ne lui **étaient** pas **dirigées**. These insults **were** not **aimed** at him/her.

6 - To head (for), to make one's way (towards)

> ➤ La voiture **se dirigeait** vers la grande place. The car **was heading** for the main square.
> ➤ Il faudrait **se diriger** dans cette direction-là. This is the course of action we need **to head** for.
> ➤ Ils **se dirigent** vers le centre-ville. They **are heading** for/**making their way** towards the town centre.
> ➤ Nous **nous sommes** tout de suite **dirigés** vers la cuisine. We immediately **headed** for/**made our way** towards the kitchen.

DISPARAÎTRE

1 - To disappear, to vanish

- ➤ Est-ce que sa cicatrice **a** entièrement **disparu? Has** his/her scar completely **disappeared?**
- ➤ Il **a disparu** tout de suite après le scandale. He **disappeared/vanished** straight after the scandal.
- ➤ La petite maison **avait disparu** dans le brouillard. The little house **had disappeared/had vanished** in the fog.
- ➤ Tous ses bijoux **ont disparu.** All his/her jewellery **has disappeared/has vanished.**

2 - To go missing, to disappear, to vanish

- ➤ Ses deux chiens **avaient disparu** deux jours après. His/her two dogs **had gone missing** two days later.
- ➤ De plus en plus d'adolescents **disparaissent** de cette région. More and more teenagers **go missing** from that area.
- ➤ Qu'est-ce qui **a disparu?** What **has gone missing/has disappeared?**
- ➤ Mon alliance **a disparu** de la coiffeuse de l'hôtel. My wedding ring **has gone missing/has vanished** from the hotel's dressing table.

3 - To die, to die out

> A l'aube elle **disparaissait**. She **died** at dawn.
> C'est une personne inoubliable qui vient de **disparaître**. Someone unforgettable has just **died**.
> Cette coutume **a disparu** il a de nombreuses années. This custom **died out** many years ago.
> Je ne voudrais pas que cette tradition **disparaisse** un jour. I wouldn't like that tradition **to die out** one day.

DISPOSER - SE DISPOSER

1 - To arrange, to set, to lay

> Comment voulez-vous que nous **disposions** les plats sur la table? How would you like us **to arrange/to set/to lay** the dishes on the table?
> Elle **a** bien **disposé** les roses dans les vases comme d'habitude. As usual she **has arranged** the roses in the vases beautifully.
> Qui **avait disposé** les meubles dans cette chambre? Who **had arranged** the furniture in this bedroom?
> J'ai préféré **disposer** les bibelots en demi-cercle. I chose **to arrange/to set** the ornaments in a semi-circle.

2 - To prepare (to), to persuade

> Alors que nous **nous disposions** à faire les bagages ils ont téléphoné. As we **prepared** to pack they phoned.
> Qu'est-ce qui pourrait **vous disposer** à le faire? What would **persuade** you to do it?
> Pense-t-il que cela les **disposerait** à payer? Does he think that it **would persuade** them to pay?
> Tout cela ne nous **a** guère **disposés** à accepter leur offre. All that **did** not really **persuade** us to accept their offer.

3 - To have at one's disposal

> Je n'**ai** jamais **disposé** d'assez de temps. I **have** never **had** enough time **at my disposal**.
> Il **dispose** de trois voitures. He **has** three cars **at his disposal**.
> Vous **disposiez** de combien d'argent? How much money **did** you **have at your disposal**?
> Cela dépendra des moyens dont nous **disposerons**. It will depend on what means we **will have at our disposal**.

4 - To go/to leave (only when giving permission to do so).

DOUBLER - SE DOUBLER

1 - To double

> Pouvez-vous **doubler** la quantité? Can you **double** the quantity?
> La compagnie **a doublé** son capital en moins d'un an. The company **has doubled** its capital in less than one year.
> Il vaudrait mieux **doubler** l'épaisseur. It would be better **to double** the thickness.
> Le nombre de licenciés risque de **doubler**. The number of people made redundant could **double**.

2 - To line

> Je vais **doubler** cette jupe. I am going **to line** this skirt.
> La boîte **est doublée** de velours rouge. The box **is lined** with red velvet.
> Les rideaux ne **sont** pas **doublés**. The curtains **are** not **lined**.
> Son manteau **est doublé** de soie. His/her coat **is lined** with silk.

3 - To overtake.

> Quand est-ce que tu vas **doubler** ce camping-car?
> When are you going **to overtake** this motorhome?
> Il ne faut jamais **doubler** dans un tournant. You must never **overtake** on a bend.
> Toutes les voitures nous **ont doublés**. All the cars **have overtaken** us.
> J'ai peur de **doubler** sur l'autoroute. I am scared of **overtaking** on the motorway.

4 - To dub

> Est-ce que le film **est doublé** en anglais? **Is** the film **dubbed** in English?
> Ce feuilleton anglais **est doublé** en plusieurs langues. This English soap opera **is dubbed** in several languages.
> Préférez-vous que le film **soit doublé** ou sous-titré? Do you prefer the film **to be dubbed** or with sub-titles?
> Le film n'**était** pas **doublé**. The film **was** not **dubbed**.

5 - To repeat (a year at school).

DRESSER - SE DRESSER

1 - To draw up, to make out, to arrange

> ➤ Ils **avaient dressé** un bon plan. They **had drawn up** a good plan.
> ➤ **Dressons** une liste de noms ensemble. Let's **draw up** a list of names together.
> ➤ Qui pourra **dresser** un tableau de service? Who will be able **to make out** a roster?
> ➤ Le couvert **a été** très bien **dressé** vous ne trouvez pas? The table settings **have been** well **arranged** don't you think?

2 - To put up, to erect, to set up

> ➤ On **a dressé** la vieille tente avec beaucoup de mal. We **have put** the old tent **up** with a lot of trouble.
> ➤ Ils **avaient dressé** des drapeaux pour l'occasion. They **had put up/had erected** some flags for the occasion.
> ➤ Une statue du politicien **sera dressée** devant la mairie. A statue of the politician **will be put up/will be erected** in front of the town hall.
> ➤ Allez **dresser** ça ailleurs. Go and **put** that **up** somewhere else.

3 - To set (against)

- Elle **a été dressée** contre moi. She **has been set** against me.
- Il ne faut pas le **dresser** contre eux. We mustn't **set** him against them.
- Ils nous **ont dressés** contre le voisin. They **set us** against the neighbour.
- Il semble aimer **dresser** les gens les uns contre les autres. It seems that he likes **setting** people against one another.

4 - To lift, to prick up (ears)

- Quand elle **a dressé** la tête j'ai vu qu'elle pleurait. When she **lifted** her face I saw that she was crying.
- **Dresse** la tête. **Lift** your head **up**.
- J'**ai dressé** l'oreille tant que j'ai pu mais je n'ai rien entendu d'intéressant. I **pricked** my ears **up** as much as I could but I didn't hear anything interesting.
- On a remarqué que le chien **avait dressé** les oreilles. We noticed that the **dog had pricked up** his ears.

5 - To train (animals)

- Elle adore **dresser** les chevaux. She loves **training** horses.

➤ On ne **dresse** plus les animaux pour le cirque. Animals **are** no longer **trained** for circus work anymore.

➤ Il n'est pas normal d'essayer de **dresser** un animal sauvage. It is not normal to try and **train** a wild animal.

➤ Ton chien **est** le mieux **dressé** que je connaisse. Your dog **is** the best **trained** dog that I know.

6 - To get up, to stand up

➤ Lorsqu'il est entré nous **nous sommes** automatiquement **dressés**. When he got in we automatically **got up**.

➤ **Dresse**-toi allons. Come on **get up/stand up**.

➤ La colline **se dresse** au milieu des maisons. The hill **stands** in the middle of the houses.

➤ L'escabeau n'**est** pas bien **dressé**. The stepladder **is** not **standing up** properly.

7 - To rise up (against): reflexive form.

ÉLEVER - S'ÉLEVER

1 - To bring up, to raise, to breed

- ➢ Elle **avait élevé** les enfants toute seule. She **had brought up** the children on her own.
- ➢ Il **a été élevé** sévèrement. He **has been** strictly **brought up**.
- ➢ **Élever** des gosses est un travail important. **Raising** children is a very important job.
- ➢ Nous **élevons** des chiens depuis presque quinze ans. We **have been breeding** dogs for almost fifteen years.

2 - To put up, to erect, to raise

- ➢ Des murs **seront élevés** autour du jardin public. Some wall **will be put up/will be erected** around the park.
- ➢ La ville voudrait **élever** un petit monument à côté de l'église. The town would like **to erect** a small monument next to the church.
- ➢ On va demander la permission d'**élever** le bâtiment. We are going to ask permission **to raise** the building.
- ➢ Il n'est pas possible d'**élever** le garage. It is not possible **to raise** the garage.

3 - To raise, to upgrade, to increase

- Pourquoi **élever** la voix? Why **raise** your voice?
- Il est défendu d'**élever** la voix dans ce lieu sacré. It is forbidden **to raise** your voice in this sacred place.
- Il voudrait **être élevé** au poste supérieur maintenant. He would like **to be upgraded** to the next level now.
- Je me suis senti **élevé** dans son estime. I felt that his esteem for me **had increased**.

4 - To rise, to go up

- Les prix vont encore **s'élever**. Prices are going **to rise** again.
- La température **s'élèvera** demain. Temperatures **will rise** tomorrow.
- Nous avons regardé l'avion **s'élever** dans le ciel. We watched the plane **go up** in the sky.
- Le niveau de l'eau de la rivière **s'élève** tous les hivers. The level of the river **goes up** every winter.

5 - To amount, to add up, to come (to a price)

- Les dommages **s'élèvent** à 2000 €. The damages **amount** to 2000 €.
- La facture **s'élève** à combien? How much **does** the invoice **amount** to?

- ➢ Les frais **se sont élevés** au double du montant prévu.
  The expenses **added up** to double the expected amount.
- ➢ Le coût des matériaux **s'élève** à 3000 €. The cost of the
  materials **comes** to 3000 €.

6 - To ascend, to fly up: reflexive form.

7 - To arise: reflexive form.

EMPRUNTER

1 - To borrow

- ➢ N'**emprunte** jamais d'argent à tes amis. Never **borrow**
  money from your friends.
- ➢ Puis-je **emprunter** vos ciseaux? Can I **borrow** your
  scissors?
- ➢ Qu'est-ce qu'il veut **emprunter**? What does he want **to
  borrow**?
- ➢ Elle **avait emprunté** des couvertures. She **had
  borrowed** some blankets.

2 - To use, to adopt

➤ Pourquoi **emprunter** un langage grossier? Why **use/adopt** a foul language?

➤ C'était amusant lorsqu'il **a emprunté** un accent pointu. It was funny when he **adopted** a posh accent.

➤ Je ne veux pas que tu **empruntes** des mots comme ça. I don't want you **to use** words like these.

➤ Elle **avait emprunté** mon idée pour sa dissertation. She **had used** my idea for her essay.

3 - To take, to follow (a route)

➤ Nous **emprunterons** le sentier. We **will take/will follow** the footpath.

➤ Le chemin qui borde le canal **est emprunté** par de nombreux cyclistes. Loads of cyclists **take/follow** the track alongside the canal.

➤ Quelle route **ont**-ils **emprunté**? Which way **did** they **take**?

➤ Beaucoup de touristes **empruntent** ce raccourci. Many tourists **take** this shortcut.

ENGAGER - S'ENGAGER

1 - To bind, to commit

- ➤ Cela ne les **engagerait** à rien. That **would** not **bind** them to anything.
- ➤ Il ne veut pas **s'engager** pour le moment. He doesn't want **to commit** himself at the moment.
- ➤ Je **me suis engagé** à le faire avant la fin du mois. I **have committed** myself to do it by the end of the month.
- ➤ Nous ne pourrons **nous engager** qu'à partir de vendredi. We will only be able **to commit** ourselves from Friday.

2 - To take on, to hire

- ➤ Ils avaient décidé d'**engager** trois ouvriers. They had decided **to take on/to hire** three workmen.
- ➤ Il les **a engagés** la semaine passée. He **took** them **on** last week.
- ➤ Combien de personnes comptez-vous **engager**? How many people do you intend **to take on/to hire**?
- ➤ Ils ne veulent pas l'**engager**. They don't want **to take** him/her **on**.

3 - To get involved

> Nous **nous engagerons** dans la politique. We **will get involved** in politics.
> Il ne faut pas **vous engager** dans leurs affaires. You mustn't **get involved** in their business.
> Elle n'aura pas peur de **s'engager** dans le débat. She won't be afraid **to get involved** in the argument.
> Pourquoi **vous étiez**-vous **engagé** dans cette discussion? Why **had** you **got involved** in the discussion?

4 - To urge, to encourage

> Il nous **a engagés** à la plus grande prudence. He **urged** us to be very very cautious.
> Elle m'**avait engagé** à parler. She **had urged** me to speak.
> Je les **ai engagés** à continuer. I **urged/encouraged** them to continue.
> Vous l'**auriez engagé** à commencer? **Would** you **have encouraged** him/her to start?

5 - To insert, to put (in)

> Veuillez **engager** votre carte dans la machine. Please **insert** your card in the machine.

> Où faut-il **engager** la clé? Where does one **insert** the key?
> Une fois la carte **engagée** tapez votre code personnel. Once the card **is inserted** key in your personal code.
> Lisez les instructions avant d'**engager** votre ticket (dans la machine) SVP. Please read the instructions before **inserting** your ticket (in the machine).

6 - To get under way, to start, to open

> La réunion **s'est engagée** dans une atmosphère agréable. The meeting got under way in a enjoyable atmosphere.
> Qui voudrait **engager** la conversation? Who would like **to start** the conversation?
> Cela risquerait d'**engager** une mésentente. That might **start** a quarrel.
> Il faudra **engager** des pourparlers bientôt. We will have **to start/to open** negotiations soon.

7 - To pawn.

8 - To invest.

9 - To enter (a sport), to start (a sport).

10 - To take a job, to enlist (military): reflexive form.

ENTENDRE - S'ENTENDRE

1 - To hear

- ➢ Nous n'**avions** rien **entendu**. We **had** not **heard** anything.
- ➢ Votre grand-père **a** tout **entendu**. Your grandfather **heard** everything.
- ➢ Qu'**a**-t-elle **entendu**? What **did** she **hear**?
- ➢ Elles ont peur lorsqu'elles **entendent** l'orage. They are scared when they **hear** thunder.

2 - To listen to

- ➢ Elle aurait dû **entendre** raison. She should have **listened** to reason.
- ➢ À les **entendre** ils sont allés partout dans le monde. **To listen** to them they've been everywhere in the world.
- ➢ Tu m'**entends**? **Are** you **listening** to me?
- ➢ Il faut que vous **entendiez** ceci. You must **listen** to this.

3 - To understand, to know all about

> ➤ Il **s'entend** bien à l'informatique. He **understands/knows all about** computers.
> ➤ Ils ne **se sont** jamais **entendus** en mathématiques. They have never **understood** maths.
> ➤ Connais-tu quelqu'un qui **s'entende** à la mécanique? Do you know someone who **knows all about** mechanics?
> ➤ Je vous **ai entendu** mais je ne partage toujours pas votre opinion. I **understand** you but I still do not share your opinion.

4 - To intend, to mean

> ➤ Qu'**entend**-il faire maintenant? What **does** he **intend** doing now?
> ➤ Nous le ferons comme nous l'**entendons**. We shall do it how we **intend** doing it.
> ➤ J'**entendais** partir vers midi. I **intended/meant** to leave around noon.
> ➤ C'est un professeur qui **entend** qu'on l'écoute. He/she is a teacher who **means** to be listened to.

5 - To get on, to agree

> ➤ Tu **t'entends** bien avec tes sœurs? Do you **get on** well with your sisters?

> ➤ Nous **nous sommes** toujours bien **entendus**. We **have** always **got on** well.
> ➤ Il ne **s'est** jamais **entendu** avec cet individu dans le bureau. He **has** never **got on** with this man in the office.
> ➤ On n'a pas réussi à **s'entendre** sur quoi que ce soit. We haven't managed **to agree** on anything.

ENTRAÎNER - S'ENTRAÎNER

1 - To carry away, to drag away, to pull, to take

> ➤ Nous nous sommes laissés **entraîner** dans leur discussion. We let ourselves be **carried away** in their talk.
> ➤ Une autre petite barque **a été entraînée** par la marée. Another small boat **has been dragged away** by the tide.
> ➤ Il l'**avait entraîné** dans le jardin pour lui demander un service. He **had pulled** him outside in order to ask him a favour.
> ➤ Où m'**entraînez**-vous? Where **are** you **taking** me?

2 - To bring about, to lead, to influence

- ➤ Ça **a entraîné** beaucoup de problèmes? **Did** that **bring about** a lot of problems?
- ➤ C'est un présentateur qui sait entraîner ses auditeurs. He is a radio presenter who knows how **to lead** his listeners.
- ➤ Où cela nous **entraînera**-t-il? Where **will** it **lead** us?
- ➤ Faites attention ils vont sans doute essayer de vous **entraîner**. Be careful they are probably going to try **to influence** you.

3 - To train, to coach

- ➤ Je **m'entraîne** à la course tous les jours. I **train** and go jogging every day.
- ➤ Tu **t'es entraîné** pendant combien de temps? How long **did** you **train** for?
- ➤ Nous devrions **nous entraîner** régulièrement. We should **train** regularly.
- ➤ Quand commencerez-vous à les **entraîner**? When will you start **training/coaching** them?

ENTRETENIR - S'ENTRETENIR

1 - To maintain, to keep up, to be serviced

> Leur caravane **a** toujours **été** mal **entretenue**. Their caravan **has** always **been** badly **maintained**.
> Ça **s'entretient** assez facilement à mon avis. In my opinion it **is** easily **maintained**.
> Nous **avons entretenu** le jardin nous-mêmes pendant vingt-cinq ans. We **kept** the garden **up** ourselves for twenty-five years.
> Quand est-ce que le chauffage central **a été entretenu**? When **was** the central heating **serviced**?

2 - To foster, to keep, to hold on to

> Il ne faut pas **entretenir** une telle émotion. You mustn't **foster** such emotions.
> **Entretenez** toutes ces pensées négatives et vous allez vous faire des cheveux blancs. If you carry on **fostering** such negative thoughts you'll get grey hair.
> Depuis quand **entretient**-il cette amitié? How long **has** he **been keeping** this friendship for?
> Pourquoi ne pas continuer à **entretenir** le même espoir? Why not continue **to hold on to** the same hope?

3 - To talk, to have a discussion

- ➤ Nous les **avions entretenus** tout le matin. We **had talked** to them all morning.
- ➤ Sur quoi allez-vous **vous entretenir** exactement? What are you going **to talk** about exactly?
- ➤ Ils **s'entretiendront** sur ce sujet dans trois jours. They **will have a discussion** about this topic in three days time.
- ➤ Nous **nous entretiendrons** sur cela cet après-midi. We **will have a discussion** about that this afternoon.

4 - To support

- ➤ C'est le fils aîné qui **entretient** toute la famille. It is the eldest son who **supports** the whole family.
- ➤ Je ne peux plus l'**entretenir**. I can't **support** him/her any more.
- ➤ Elle **a été entretenue** par son ami pendant dix ans. Her boyfriend **supported** her for ten years.
- ➤ Ils ne veulent pas que vous les **entreteniez**. They don't want you **to support** them.

ESTIMER - S'ESTIMER

1 - To value, to assess, to estimate

> ➤ Elles ont voulu faire **estimer** le collier en or de leur grand-mère. They wanted to have their grandmother's gold necklace **valued**.
> ➤ Ils ont l'intention de faire **estimer** leur propriété. They plan to have their property **valued**.
> ➤ Le tableau **a été estimé** à une valeur de 4000 €. The painting **has been valued** at 4000 €.
> ➤ Le nombre de blessés est difficile à **estimer** pour le moment. The number of people injured is difficult **to assess/to estimate** yet.

2 - To respect, to appreciate, to value

> ➤ Nous n'**avons** jamais beaucoup **estimé** leur père. We **have** never **respected** their father very much.
> ➤ C'est une dame que j'**estime** beaucoup. She is a lady I **do respect** a lot.
> ➤ Êtes-vous **estimé** par vos collègues? **Are** you **respected/appreciated/valued** by your colleagues?
> ➤ Le vin français **est** énormément **estimé** dans le monde. French wine **is** greatly **respected/appreciated/valued** in the world.

3 - To consider, to reckon, to judge

> ➤ On **estimait** que c'était une obligation. We **considered** that it was an obligation.
> ➤ Ils **s'estiment** assez heureux. They **consider themselves** quite happy.
> ➤ Tu **estimes** que c'est vraiment nécessaire? **Do** you **reckon** that it is really necessary?
> ➤ Vous **avez estimé** bon de vous taire? You **judged** that it was best to say nothing?

FICHER - SE FICHER

1 - To do, to be up to (both only in questions or with 'nothing') (past participle: fichu)

> ➤ Je n'**ai** rien **fichu** hier. I **did** not **do** a thing yesterday.
> ➤ Elle n'**a** rien **fichu** de toute la semaine. She **has** not **done** a thing all week.
> ➤ Qu'est-ce que tu **fiches**? What **are** you **up to**?
> ➤ Que **fichiez**-vous là-bas? What **were** you **up to** over there?

2 - To place, to put, to stick (past participle: fiché)

> **Fichez** vos manteaux ici. **Place/put/stick** your coats here.
> Ne **fichez** pas le pain sur la chaise. Don't **place/put/stick** the bread on the chair.
> J'**ai** tout **fiché** dans le tiroir. I **placed/put/stuck** everything in the drawer.
> Elle ne sait pas où elle **a fiché** son passeport. She doesn't know where she **has put** her passport.

3 - To pull someone's leg, to take someone for a ride (past participle: fiché)

> Ne **te fiche** pas de lui tout le temps. Don't **pull his leg** all the time.
> Ils **se sont fichés** de toi. They **pulled your leg/took you for a ride**.
> Elle n'aime pas qu'on **se fiche** d'elle. She doesn't like people **to pull her leg/take her for a ride**.
> Le maçon ne **s'est** pas **fiché de nous**. The bricklayer **did** not **take us for a ride**.

4 - Not to care less: reflexive form.

FIGURER - SE FIGURER

1 - To appear, to be

- ➢ Tous leurs noms **figureront** sur une plaque en marbre. All their names **will appear/will be** on a marble plaque.
- ➢ Plusieurs de ses amis **figurent** sur la liste. Several of his/her friends **appear/are** on the list.
- ➢ Est-ce que ton nom **figure** parmi ceux qui ont contribué? **Is** your name amongst those who have contributed?
- ➢ La société ne **figure** plus dans l'annuaire. The company **is** no longer in the telephone directory.

2 - To imagine, to think, to believe

- ➢ **Figure-toi** une pièce avec vue sur ce lac. **Imagine** a room with a view on this lake.
- ➢ Vous ne pourrez jamais **vous figurer** combien il me manque. You will never be able **to imagine** how much I miss him.
- ➢ Il **s'était figuré** qu'il était le seul à penser ça. He **thought/believed** that he was the only one to think that.
- ➢ **Figurez-**vous qu'il s'agissait seulement d'une plaisanterie! **Would** you **believe** that it was only a joke!

FORMER - SE FORMER

1 - To make, to create, to be in the shape of

> ➢ Cela ne **forme** pas un tout. That doesn't **make** a whole.
> ➢ Nous **formerons** un nouveau projet avant février. We **will make** a new plan by February.
> ➢ Qui **avait formé** cette compagnie? Who **had created** this company?
> ➢ Le nouveau sentier **formera** plusieurs grandes boucles. The new footpath **will be in the shape of** several large circles.

2 - To train, to develop, to broaden

> ➢ Il avait préféré **se former** sur le tas. He chose **to train** on the job.
> ➢ Je suis chargé de les **former** avant Pâques. It is my responsibility **to train** them before Easter.
> ➢ Ça **forme** l'esprit. It **develops/broadens** the mind.
> ➢ Le voyage est un bon moyen pour **former** le caractère. Travelling is a good way **to develop/to broaden** one's character.

FUIR

1 - To avoid, to shun

- ➢ J'ai toujours **fui** ce genre de choses. I **have** always **avoided** that kind of things.
- ➢ Que **fuit**-il exactement? What exactly **is** he **avoiding**?
- ➢ Pourquoi est-ce que ton chien me **fuit** aujourd'hui? Why is your dog **avoiding** me today?
- ➢ C'est quelqu'un qui les **a** continuellement **fuis**. He is someone who **has** repeatedly **shunned** them.

2 - To flee, to run away, to escape

- ➢ Les soldats **ont fui** à temps. The soldiers **fled** in time.
- ➢ Il a dit qu'il **fuirait**. He said that he **would run away**.
- ➢ Ils **ont fui** ensemble. They **fled/ran away/escaped** together.
- ➢ Vous avez tous réussi à **fuir**? Did you all manage **to escape**?

3 - To leak

> ➤ Ce robinet **fuit** depuis trois jours. This tap **has been leaking** for three days.
> ➤ Est-ce que le tuyau **a fui**? **Did** the pipe **leak**?
> ➤ Ton stylo **fuit** un peu. Your pen **is leaking** a little.
> ➤ Quelque chose **avait fui** dans la cave. Something **had leaked** in the cellar.

GAGNER

1 - To earn, to gain

> ➤ Si j'accepte je **gagnerai** beaucoup plus que maintenant. If I accept I **will earn** a lot more than I do at present.
> ➤ Il **gagnait** tout juste assez pour vivre. He **used to earn** just about enough to live on.
> ➤ Qu'**avez**-vous **gagné** à faire ça? What **did** you **gain** by doing this?
> ➤ Elle **gagnera** pas mal de temps. She **will gain** a fair amount of time.

2 - To win

- ➢ Nous **avons gagné**. We **won**.
- ➢ Je voudrais qu'elle **gagne**. I would love her **to win**.
- ➢ Il **gagnait** à chaque fois. He **used to win** each time.
- ➢ Il faut savoir **gagner** la confiance d'autrui. You have **to win** people's trust.

3 - To get better, to improve

- ➢ Normalement le vin **gagne** à vieillir. Normally wine **gets better/improves** with time.
- ➢ Pour moi le film **gagne** à être revu. In my opinion the film **gets better/improves** the second time you watch it.
- ➢ Peut-être **gagneraient**-ils à être mieux connus. Maybe they **would get better/would improve** if one got to know them a bit more.
- ➢ Ajoutez un peu de basilic et le plat y **gagnera** en saveur. The (taste of the) dish **will improve** by adding a little basil.

4 - To reach, to spread

- ➢ Malheureusement l'incendie **avait gagné** la ferme avant l'arrivée des pompiers. Sadly the fire **had reached** the farm before the fire brigade arrived.

➢ Il compte **gagner** le sommet avant quatre heures. He plans **to reach** the top before four.

➢ La nouvelle les **gagnera** tôt ou tard. The news **will reach** them sooner or later.

➢ Tout à coup j'**ai été gagné** par une grande peur. Panic **spread** all over me unexpectedly.

GARDER - SE GARDER

1 - To look after, to mind

➢ Pourriez-vous **garder** ma petite-fille cet après-midi? Could you **look after** my granddaughter this afternoon?

➢ C'était toujours ma tante qui **gardait** mes chats. It was always my aunt who **looked after** my cats.

➢ Qui **a gardé** les malades? Who **looked after** the patients?

➢ Tu peux me **garder** mon sac? Could you **look after/mind** my bag?

2 - To keep, to put aside

➢ Il **a été gardé** à l'hôpital toute la journée. He **has been kept** at the hospital the whole day.

➢ Ils voudraient nous **garder** ici. They would like **to keep** us here.

> ➤ Est-ce que tu leur **avais gardé** des places? **Had** you **put** some tickets **aside** for them?
> ➤ Pourriez-vous lui **garder** une brochure? Could you **put** a brochure **aside** for him/her?

3 - To avoid, to be weary, to beware, to refrain

> ➤ Si j'étais toi je **me garderais** bien de lui parler. If I were you I **would avoid** talking to him/her.
> ➤ De qui **vous gardez**-vous? Who **are** you **weary of**?
> ➤ Nous **nous gardons** des flatteurs. We **beware** of people who praise people.
> ➤ Elle **s'est gardée** de nous dire ça. She **refrained** from telling us.

4 - To stay (in bed or in bedroom)

> ➤ Il va lui falloir **garder** le lit pendant plusieurs jours. He/she is going to have **to stay** in bed for several days.
> ➤ Il a fallu la forcer à **garder** le lit. We had to force her **to stay** in bed.
> ➤ Il n'**avait gardé** le lit que deux jours. He **had** only **stayed** in bed for two days.
> ➤ Pourquoi est-ce que tu **as gardé** la chambre si longtemps? Why **did** you **stay** in your room for so long?

5 - To keep, to retain.

GÊNER - SE GÊNER

1 - To bother, to put (someone) out, to be in the way

> Il ne voulait pas nous **gêner**. He didn't want **to bother** us.
> Je suis sûr que cela ne la **gênera** pas du tout. I am sure that it **will** not **bother** her at all.
> J'espère que je ne vous **gêne** pas. I hope that I **am** not **putting** you **out**.
> Si vous vous garez ici vous allez **gêner** la circulation. If you park here you are going **to be in the way** of the traffic.

2 - To embarrass, to make uncomfortable

> Il nous **a gênés** devant mes amis. He **embarrassed** us in front of my friends.
> Vous avez dit ça pour la **gêner**? Did you say that **to embarrass** her?
> Pourquoi **étais**-tu si **gêné**? Why **were** you so **embarrassed**?
> Je veux que personne ne **se gêne** ici faites comme chez vous. I don't want anyone **to be uncomfortable** here make yourselves at home.

3 - To put in financial difficulties.

HEURTER - SE HEURTER

1 - To hit, to collide

- ➢ Il **s'est heurté** à la porte en tombant. He **hit** the door whilst falling over.
- ➢ Attention de ne pas **te heurter** la tête. Mind you don't **hit** your head.
- ➢ Un camion **a heurté** notre arbre. A lorry **hit** our tree.
- ➢ Nos voitures **se sont heurtées**. Our cars **collided**.

2 - To offend, to clash, to upset

- ➢ Je ne veux pas **heurter** qui que ce soit. I don't want **to offend** anybody at all.
- ➢ Vous allez les **heurter**. You are going **to offend/upset** them.
- ➢ Cette remarque les **avait** beaucoup **heurtés**. This comment **had** greatly **upset** them.
- ➢ Nos opinions **se heurtent** chaque fois. Our views **clash** each time.

IGNORER - S'IGNORER

1 - To ignore

> Il m'**a** encore **ignoré**. He ignored me again.
> Elles **s'ignorent** depuis hier. They **have been ignoring each other** since yesterday.
> Pourquoi **avez**-vous **ignoré** mon conseil? Why **did** you **ignore** my advice?
> Ils n'auraient jamais dû **ignorer** ces avertissements. They should never have **ignored** these warnings.

2 - To be unaware, not to know

> Vous **ignoriez** qu'il était suisse? You **were not aware/didn't know** that he was Swiss?
> Elle **ignorait** que j'étais malade. She **was unaware/did not know** that I was ill.
> Elles pensent que leur oncle **ignore** tous les détails. They think that their uncle **does not know** all the details.
> Nous avons dit que nous **ignorions** où il habite. We said that we **did not know** where he lived.

IMPORTER

1 - To import, to introduce

➤ Le pays **importe** du café. The country **imports** some coffee.

➤ Les marchandises **seront importées** le mois prochain. The goods **will be imported** next month.

➤ Ils **ont importé** du mimosa pendant une trentaine d'années. They **imported** mimosa for about thirty years.

➤ Le pays **a importé** cette coutume française il y a au moins un demi-siècle. The country **introduced** this French habit at least half a century ago.

2 - To matter, to be necessary, to be important

➤ C'est ce qui **importe** le plus. That's what **matters** the most.

➤ Qu'**importe**! What **does** it **matter**!

➤ Il **importe** de leur répondre immédiatement. It **is necessary/is important** to reply to them immediately.

➤ Ce qui **importe** c'est d'essayer de comprendre. What **matters/is necessary/is important** is to try and understand.

INTRODUIRE - S'INTRODUIRE

1 - To get in, to put in, to insert

> ➢ Ils **s'y sont introduits** sans être questionnés. They **got in** there without being asked anything.
> ➢ Un cambrioleur **s'est introduit** dans l'école pendant la nuit. A thief **got in** the school in the night.
> ➢ Je ne sais quelle clé il faut **introduire**. I don't know which key I have **to put in**.
> ➢ **Introduisez** votre carte une deuxième fois. **Insert** your card a second time.

2 - To show (in/into)

> ➢ N'**introduisez** personne dans cette pièce avant 11 heures. Don't **show** anyone into this room until 11 o'clock.
> ➢ Il **sera introduit** dans son bureau. He **will be shown** into his/her office.
> ➢ Elle l'**introduira** dans la salle d'attente. She **will show** him/her **into** the waiting room.
> ➢ Il **a introduit** les dames dans l'appartement une à une. He **showed** the ladies **in** the flat one by one.

3 - To introduce, to launch

> ➤ Qui **avait introduit** cette idée-là? Who **had introduced** that idea?
> ➤ Cette mode **a été introduite** voilà plus de dix ans. This fashion **was introduced** more than ten years ago.
> ➤ Cette expression **a été introduite** dans la langue française après la guerre. This expression **was introduced** in the French language after the war.
> ➤ Il compte **introduire** son propre label l'hiver prochain. He intends **to launch** his own designer label next winter.

4 - To put someone in contact with someone.

JOINDRE - SE JOINDRE

1 - To join, to put together

> ➤ Et si on **joignait** deux bouts de ficelle? What if we **joined** two pieces of string?
> ➤ Ils **avaient joint** leurs lits. They **had put** their beds **together**.
> ➤ Trois tables **étaient jointes** pour le buffet. Three tables **were put together** for the buffet.
> ➤ **Joignez** les mains pendant les prières. **Put your hands together** when you pray.

2 - To link

- ➤ Il y a une chaussée qui **joint** l'île à la ville lorsque la marée est basse. There is a causeway that **links** the island to the town when the tide is low.
- ➤ Le tunnel **joindra** les deux pays. The tunnel **will link** the two countries.
- ➤ Ils parlent de **joindre** l'île au continent par un câble. They are talking about **linking** the island to the mainland by cable.
- ➤ Avant il y avait un petit pont qui **joignait** les deux bâtiments. There used to be a little bridge that **used to link** the two buildings.

3 - To combine, to unite, to get together

- ➤ Il a toujours su comment **joindre** l'utile à l'agréable. He has always had the knack **to combine** business with pleasure.
- ➤ On aura plus de chance de réussir en **joignant** nos efforts. We will have more chance of succeeding by **combining** our efforts.
- ➤ Le maire **a joint** en mariage le premier couple homosexuel. The mayor **united** the first homosexual couple in marriage.
- ➤ Ils ne veulent pas **se joindre** à nous. They don't want **to get together** with us.

4 - To add, to attach, to enclose

> ➤ J'ai oublié de **joindre** mon chèque à la lettre. I forgot **to add/to attach** my cheque to the letter.
> ➤ Que dois-je **joindre** d'autre? What else do I have **to add/to attach**?
> ➤ Il n'y avait aucun autre renseignement **joint** au dossier. There was no other information **added/attached** to the file.
> ➤ Veuillez trouver ci-**joint** la photo demandée. The required photograph **is enclosed**.

5 - To contact, to get in touch

> ➤ Comment pourrons-nous vous **joindre**? How will we be able **to contact** you?
> ➤ L'hôpital essaie de **joindre** son plus proche parent. The hospital is trying **to contact** his/her next of kin.
> ➤ Je l'**ai joint** au téléphone en fin de soirée. I **got in touch** with him on the phone late in the evening.
> ➤ Voici l'adresse où les **joindre**. This is the address where you can **get in touch** with them.

6 - To shut, to close (with windows or doors as subjects).

LÂCHER

1 - To let go, to drop

➤ Ne lui **lâche** pas la main. Don't **let go** of his/her hand.
➤ **Lâche**-moi. **Let go** of me.
➤ Elle **avait** tout **lâché**. She **had dropped** everything.
➤ Ne **lâchez** pas le paquet. Don't **drop** the parcel.

2 - To abandon

➤ Pourquoi nous **lâcheraient**-ils? Why **would** they **abandon** us?
➤ J'avais décidé de **lâcher** mes études. I had decided **to abandon** my studies.
➤ Il n'est pas question de **lâcher** le projet maintenant. It is out of question **to abandon** the project now.
➤ Tu ne vas pas tout **lâcher** après tout ce temps! You are not going **to abandon** everything after all this time!

3 - To loosen, to let out, to come off

➤ **Lâche** un peu la corde c'est trop tiré. **Loosen** the rope a bit it's too tight.

> Il faudrait **lâcher** la taille de ton pantalon. You should **let** the waist of your trousers **out**.
> La couturière **a lâché** les coutures de la robe de mariée car la cliente avait un peu grossi. The dressmaker **let** the seams of the wedding dress **out** because the customer had put on a bit of weight.
> Le bandage n'est pas assez serré il va **lâcher**. The bandage is not tight enough it is going **to come off**.

4 - To break, to give way

> On t'avait dit que l'élastique allait **lâcher**. We told you that the elastic was going **to break**.
> La passerelle **avait lâché**. The footbridge **had given way**.
> Le plafond **a lâché**. The ceiling **gave way**.
> J'ai peur que cette étagère ne **lâche** sous le poids des livres. I am worried in case this shelf **gives way** under the weight of the books.

5 - To come out with (something stupid or rude).

LANCER - SE LANCER

1 - To throw

- ➢ Les enfants **lançaient** des cailloux dans l'eau. The children **were throwing** pebbles in the water.
- ➢ Arrêtez de **lancer** les choses. Stop **throwing** things.
- ➢ **Lance**-lui la serviette. **Throw** him/her the towel.
- ➢ Je lui ai demandé de me **lancer** le journal. I asked him/her **to throw** me the newspaper.

2 - To shout

- ➢ Il leur **lançait** des insultes de sa fenêtre. He **used to shout** insults at them from his window.
- ➢ Elle m'**a lancé** quelques mots grossiers. She **shouted** a few swear words at me.
- ➢ Ils nous **ont lancé** un bonjour en passant. They **shouted** hello as they went by.
- ➢ A l'intention de qui **avait**-il **lancé** ces paroles? Who **had** he **shouted** these words at?

3 - To launch, to get (into a venture)

- ➢ Ce parfum **a été lancé** il y a plus de trois ans. This perfume **was launched** over three years ago.
- ➢ Qui **avait lancé** cette mode? Who **had launched** this fashion?
- ➢ Un des plus célèbres acteurs français **avait lancé** la carrière de cette chanteuse. One of the most famous French actors **had launched** this singer's career.
- ➢ Vous avez décidé de **vous lancer** dans le tourisme? **Have** you decided **to get** into tourism?

4 - To leap, to jump

- ➢ A la fin du film le car **se lance** dans le vide. At the end of the film the coach **leaps** into space.
- ➢ Il y a deux témoins l'ont vu **se lancer** sur la personne âgée. There are two witnesses who saw him **jump** on the elderly man/woman.
- ➢ J'ai pleuré quand le lion **s'est lancé** sur sa proie. I cried when I saw the lion **jump** on his prey.
- ➢ Les parachutistes **se sont lancés** à tour de rôle. The parachutists **jumped** in turn.

5 - To project (smoke).

6 - To build up speed: reflexive form.

LIVRER - SE LIVRER

1 - To deliver

- L'armoire **sera livrée** mercredi. The wardrobe **will be delivered** on Wednesday.
- Nous ne **livrons** pas le samedi. We do not **deliver** on Saturdays.
- Rien n'**a été livré**. Nothing **has been delivered**.
- Où voulez-vous que nous **livrions** votre commande? Where do you want us **to deliver** your order?

2 - To hand over, to give away, to reveal

- Ne me **livre** pas à la police. Don't **hand** me **over** to the police.
- Le groupe de réfugiés **a été livré** aux autorités il y a une heure. The group of refugees **has been handed over** to the authorities one hour ago.
- Elle ne **livrera** jamais son secret pour cette recette. She **will** never **give away** her secret for this recipe.
- Il ne **s'est** jamais **livré** à personne. He **has** never **revealed** himself to anyone.

3 - To indulge, to practise, to devote

➢ Depuis quand **se livre**-t-il au jeu? How long **has** he **been indulging** in gambling for?

➢ Elle a toujours voulu **se livrer** entièrement à la religion. She has always wanted **to devote herself** completely to religion.

➢ Il est nécessaire que nous **nous livrions** à ces recherches supplémentaires. It is necessary that we **devote ourselves** to this further research.

➢ Vous pourrez **vous livrer** à un grand nombre de sports pendant votre séjour ici. You will be able **to practise** a good many sports during your stay here.

LOUER

1 - To praise, to congratulate

> Elle **loue** son petit-fils à longueur de temps. She can't stop **praising** her grandson.
> Leur professeur les **a loués** devant tous les autres. Their teacher **praised/congratulated** them in front of all the others.
> Ils ne peuvent que **se louer** d'avoir fait cela. They can only **congratulate themselves** to have done what they did.
> Il faut **louer** Dieu quotidiennement. You have **to praise** God every day.

2 - To let, to rent, to hire

> Tu **avais loué** une voiture pour combien de temps? How long **had** you **hired** a car for?
> Nous pourrions **louer** notre résidence secondaire pendant le printemps. We could **let** our holiday home for the spring.
> Où peut-on **louer** des vélos? Where can one **hire** bicycles?
> Ils ont l'intention de **louer** un camping car. They plan **to hire** a motorhome.

MARCHER

1 - To walk

> ➢ Ils **marcheront** toute la journée. They **will walk** the whole day.
> ➢ **Marchez** plus vite. **Walk** faster.
> ➢ Vous **avez marché** où? Where **did** you **walk**?
> ➢ Il faut que nous **marchions** davantage c'est bon pour la santé. We must **walk** more it's good for health.

2 - To step

> ➢ Ne **marchez** pas sur ça. Don't **step** on that.
> ➢ Faites attention de ne pas **marcher** dans la boue. Be careful not **to step** in the mud.
> ➢ Il a fait exprès de me **marcher** sur le pied. He **stepped** on my foot on purpose.
> ➢ Est-ce que nous pouvons **marcher** sur les carreaux maintenant? Can we **step** on the tiles now?

3 - To work (mechanical things), to go (mechanical things)

- ➢ Sa montre ne **marche** plus. His/her watch doesn't **work** any more.
- ➢ Est-ce que votre voiture **marche** mieux? Is the car **working/going** better?
- ➢ Je suis venu à vélo parce que le métro ne **marchait** pas ce matin. I cycled here because the tube **was** not **working** this morning.
- ➢ Comment ça **marche** ce truc? How **does** that thing **work**?

4 - To be (well-not well), to go (well-not well)

- ➢ Ça **marche**? How **is** it **going**?
- ➢ Espérons que tout **marchera** bien demain. Let's hope that all **will be well/go well** tomorrow.
- ➢ Leur ménage ne **marche** pas bien en ce moment. Their marriage **is** not **going** very well at the moment.
- ➢ Comment **marche** le travail? How **is** work?

5 - To march.

6 - To stride (towards fame, success).

METTRE - SE METTRE

1 - To put

> ➤ Il vaut mieux **mettre** le pique-nique à l'ombre. We had better **put** the picnic in the shade.
> ➤ Elle **aura mis** les enfants au lit. She **will have put** the children to bed.
> ➤ Il veut **mettre** toute son énergie dans ce nouveau projet. He wants **to put** all his energy in this project.
> ➤ Où **as**-tu **mis** mon porte-monnaie? Where **have** you **put** my purse?

2 - To wear, to put on (clothes)

> ➤ Je ne sais pas ce que je vais **me mettre**. I don't know what I am going **to wear/to put on**.
> ➤ Elle n'a mis ce chapeau qu'une fois. She **has** only **worn** this hat once.
> ➤ Il n'arrive pas à **se mettre** ses chaussures. He can't manage **to put** his shoes **on**.
> ➤ Quel maillot vas-tu **te mettre**? Which swimming costume are you going **to wear**?

3 - To take (time)

- ➢ Le trajet **met** combien de temps exactement? How long **does** the journey **take** exactly?
- ➢ Le courrier **a mis** une semaine à arriver. The post **took** one week to arrive.
- ➢ Ça **mettra** moins d'une semaine. It **will take** less than one week.
- ➢ Il ne **met** que dix minutes pour se coiffer. He only **takes** ten minutes to do his hair.

4 - To start, to begin

- ➢ Il ne sait pas pourquoi il **s'est mis** à rire. He doesn't know why he **started** to laugh.
- ➢ Nous **nous mettrons** au travail après le petit-déjeuner. We **will start** work after breakfast.
- ➢ Quand comptes-tu **te mettre** à tes devoirs? When do you intend **starting** your homework?
- ➢ Chaque fois que je lave la voiture il **se met** à pleuvoir. Each time I wash the car it **starts/begins** to rain.

5 - To install, to fit, to build

- ➢ On va **mettre** une douche dans la salle de bain. We are going **to install** a shower in the bathroom.

- ➢ Où pourrait-on **mettre** une bibliothèque? Where could we **fit** a bookcase?
- ➢ Ils **ont mis** une belle cheminée dans leur salon. They **built** a lovely fireplace in the lounge.
- ➢ Il n'y a pas la place pour **mettre** deux éviers. There isn't room **to fit** two sinks.

6 - Supposing/let's suppose that (only first person plural of imperative tense)

- ➢ **Mettons** qu'il ne réponde jamais. **Supposing/let's suppose** that he never replies.
- ➢ **Mettons** que ça coûte 5000 €. **Supposing/let's suppose** that it costs 5000 €.
- ➢ **Mettons** qu'elle ait raison. **Supposing/let's suppose** that she were right.
- ➢ **Mettons** qu'ils viennent tous. **Supposing/let's suppose** that they all come.

7 - To switch on (machines).

MIJOTER

1 - To simmer, to (lovingly) cook

> ➤ Quelque chose de bon **mijotait** dans la cuisine. Something tasty **was simmering** in the kitchen.
> ➤ La viande **mijote** depuis trois heures. The meat **has been simmering** since three o'clock.
> ➤ Je leur **mijotais** leur plat préféré. I **used to lovingly cook** them their favourite dish.
> ➤ Le ragoût doit **mijoter** pendant quatre heures au minimum. The casserole has **to cook** for a minimum of four hours.

To plot

> ➤ Nous sommes sûrs qu'ils sont en train de **mijoter** quelque chose. We are sure that they **are plotting** something.
> ➤ C'est vous qui **avez mijoté** ce sale coup? Was it you who **plotted** this kick in the teeth?
> ➤ Qu'est-ce que tu **mijotes** encore? What **are** you **plotting** again?
> ➤ Elles **avaient mijoté** ça pendant toute une semaine. They **had been plotting** that for a whole week.

MONTER - SE MONTER

1 - To go up, to climb

- ➤ On **montera** au grenier. We **will go up** in the loft.
- ➤ Il **est monté** au deuxième étage. He **went up** to the second floor.
- ➤ Je **montais** le sentier quand j'ai entendu un cri. I **was going up** the footpath when I heard a scream.
- ➤ Ils **montaient** à la colline tous les dimanches. They **used to go up/used to climb** the hill every Sunday.

2 - To get (in-on means of transport)

- ➤ **Montons** dans le train il va partir. **Let's get** on the train it's about to leave.
- ➤ Ils **montaient** dans un taxi. They **were getting** in a taxi.
- ➤ A quelle heure est-ce qu'on pourra **monter** dans l'avion? At what time will we be able **to get** on the plane?
- ➤ **Montez** dans le bus maintenant. **Get** on the bus now.

3 - To be on the way up, to rise

> ➤ Ce week-end bonne nouvelle les baromètres vont **monter**. This weekend good news, the temperature is going **to rise**.
> ➤ Les prix continueraient de **monter**. Prices would continue **to rise**.
> ➤ Puis l'eau s'est arrêtée de **monter**. Then the water stopped **rising**.
> ➤ C'est un acteur qui **monte**. He is an actor (who) **is on the way up**.

4 - To come, to reach

> ➤ Ça **se montera** à combien environ? That **will come** to about how much?
> ➤ Les frais **se sont montés** au double de ce que nous avions prévu. Expenses **came** to double those we had expected.
> ➤ L'eau de la rivière ne nous **montait** qu'aux genoux. The water in the river only **reached** to our knees.
> ➤ L'encolure de cette robe du soir monte trop haut. The neckline of this evening dress **comes/reaches** too high.

5 - To take up, to bring up

- ➢ Il pourrait nous **monter** le plateau? Could he **take up** the tray for us?
- ➢ Nous **avions monté** les gosses dans leurs chambres. We **had taken** the kids **up** to their rooms.
- ➢ Quand vas-tu lui **monter** le journal? When are you going **to take up** the paper to him/her?
- ➢ Qu'est-ce qu'elle veut qu'on lui **monte**? What does she want us **to take up/to bring up**?
- ➢

6 - To set up, to organize, to put up

- ➢ Le jeune couple prend du plaisir à **se monter**. The young couple have fun **setting up** (home).
- ➢ Ils ont décidé de **monter** un complot. They decided **to set up** a plot.
- ➢ J'**avais monté** ma propre entreprise. I **had set up** my own business.
- ➢ C'est eux qui avaient voulu tout **monter**. They had wanted **to set up/to organize/to put up** everything.

7 - To go to seed (plants).

8 - To ride (a horse).

9 - To set, to mount (jewellery).

NOTER

1 - To make a note of, to write down, to note down

- ➢ Je vais **noter** votre nom et adresse tout de suite. I am going **to make a note of/to write down/to note down** your name and address straight away.
- ➢ Où **as**-tu **noté** le numéro de téléphone? Where **did** you **write down** the telephone number?
- ➢ Il **avait noté** le rendez-vous dans son agenda. He **had made a note of/had written down/had noted down** the appointment in his diary.
- ➢ Vous auriez dû **noter** l'immatriculation du véhicule. You should have **made a note of/written down/noted down** the car registration number.

2 - To note (not forget), to make a mental note of, to notice

- ➢ Est-ce que ça mérite d'être **noté**? Is that worth **noting/making a mental note of**?
- ➢ **Notez** bien ce qu'ils disent. Do **note/make a mental note** of what they are saying.
- ➢ Il n'**avait** rien **noté** de différent. He **had** not **noticed** anything different.
- ➢ Son absence n'**a** pas **été notée**? His/her absence **was** not **noticed**?

3 - To mark (mostly grades)

➢ Le professeur **a noté** une vingtaine de devoirs. The teacher **has marked** about twenty pieces of homework.
➢ Elle **avait noté** plusieurs dates possibles dans son calendrier. She **had marked** a few possible dates in her calendar.
➢ Qui **notera** son travail? Who is going **to mark** his/her work?
➢ Ma dissertation n'**a** pas encore **été notée**. My essay **has** not **been marked** yet.

NOYER - SE NOYER

1 - To drown

> Tu vas **te noyer** dans ces vagues. You are going **to drown** in these waves.

> Trois enfants **se sont noyés** dans la rivière. Three children **have drowned** in the river.

> Elle s'est suicidée en **se noyant**. She killed herself by **drowning**.

> Il **noie** son chagrin dans l'alcool. He **drowns** his sorrows in alcohol.

2 - To swamp, to lose

> Le paysage **était noyé** dans la brume. The scenery **was swamped** in the mist.

> Sa réponse **était noyée** dans un tas d'excuses. His/her reply **was lost** in a pile of excuses.

> La musique **était** complètement **noyée** par les cris des fans. The music **was** completely **lost** in the noise the fans made.

> Mes paroles **ont été noyées** dans le bruit de la circulation. My words **were lost** in the traffic noise.

3 - To water down (drink), to make too thin (sauce).

OBLIGER - S'OBLIGER

1 - To force, to make (someone do something), to require

- ➤ Ils m'**obligeaient** à y aller une fois par semaine. They **used to force/used to make** me go there once a week.
- ➤ C'est pas la peine de les **obliger**: There is no need **to force** them.
- ➤ Ça pourrait les **obliger** à changer d'avis. That could **make** them change their minds.
- ➤ C'est **obligé** de donner son nom et adresse? Are names and addresses **required**?

2 - To have (to do), to be bound, to be compelled

- ➤ Nos responsabilités nous **obligent** à accepter. We **have** to accept out of duty.
- ➤ Je me suis toujours senti **obligé** de le faire. I have always felt **bound/compelled** to do it.
- ➤ Tu n'**es** pas **obligé** de nous aider. You don't **have** to help us.
- ➤ Est-ce que nous **sommes obligés** de signer? Do we **have** to sign?

3 - To oblige, to help

> ➤ Il faut **obliger** ses amis. You have **to oblige/to help** your friends.
> ➤ Vous nous **obligeriez** si vous pouviez arriver avant le trois août. You **would oblige/would help** us if you could arrive before the third of August.
> ➤ Elle les **obligerait** si elle venait aussi. It **would help** them if she came as well.
> ➤ Je pense qu'ils t'**obligeront** volontiers. In my opinion they **will** be glad **to oblige/to help** you.

OFFRIR - S'OFFRIR

1 - To give (presents)

> ➤ Il lui **offrait** des fleurs pour son anniversaire. He **used to give** him/her some flowers for his/her birthday.
> ➤ Elle nous **avait offert** un très beau cadeau. She **had given** us a wonderful present.
> ➤ Qu'est-ce que vous leur **offrirez** cette année? What **will** you **give** them this year?
> ➤ Je ne sais pas quoi **offrir** à ma nièce. I don't know what **to give** my niece.

> ➢ **2 - To offer, to volunteer**

> ➢ **J'ai offert** de les aider après le déjeuner. I
> **offered/volunteered** to help them after lunch.
> ➢ Nous **nous étions offerts**. We **had offered**
> (ourselves)/**had volunteered**.
> ➢ Est-ce que tu leur **as offert** un verre? **Did** you **offer**
> them a drink?
> ➢ Combien **ont**-ils **offert** pour le bateau? How much **did**
> they **offer** for the boat?

3 - To present, to give

> ➢ Elle va nous **offrir** deux possibilités. She is going **to**
> **present** us with two possibilities.
> ➢ Il a une idée excellent à leur **offrir**. He has an excellent
> idea **to present** to them.
> ➢ Combien de choix vous **ont été offerts**? How many
> choices **did** they **give** you?
> ➢ Je n'ai pas d'explication à vous **offrir**. I don't have an
> explanation to give you.

4 - To treat (someone) to

> ➢ Ils vont **s'offrir** une croisière pour leurs noces d'argent.
> They are going **to treat themselves to** a cruise for their
> silver wedding anniversary.

➤ Elle **s'est offert** un lifting pour ses cinquante ans. She **treated herself to** a face-lift for her fiftieth birthday.

➤ Ils nous **offrent** l'apéritif au Bar de l' Île d'Or. They **are treating** us **to** an aperitif at the Bar de l' Île d'Or.

➤ Si je gagnais à la loterie je **m'offrirais** un diamant. If I won the lottery I **would treat myself to** a diamond.

OPÉRER - S'OPÉRER

1 - To carry out, to achieve

➤ Les travaux **seront opérés** quand? When **will** the work **be carried out**?

➤ Est-ce que tout **serait opéré** par la même compagnie? **Would** the same firm **carry** all of it **out**?

➤ Les vacances **opèrent** un bénéfice à la fois physique et mental. Holidays **achieve** both physical and mental wellbeing.

➤ Rien n'**opèrera** un tel miracle. Nothing **will achieve** such a miracle.

2 - To act, to work

- ➤ Nous **opèrerons** avec précaution. We **will act** with care.
- ➤ Après tout cela je ne sais pas comment il faudra **opérer**. After all that I don't know what the best way **to act** will be.
- ➤ Son charme ne risque pas d'**opérer** avec moi. His charm is not likely **to work** with me.
- ➤ Comment est-ce que ce système **opèrerait**? How **would** that system **work**?

3 - To operate, to do an operation

- ➤ Il est trop tard pour **opérer**. It is too late **to operate**.
- ➤ Il avait fallu **opérer** sans délai. It had been necessary **to operate/to do an operation** without delay.
- ➤ Le docteur qui l'**a opéré** n'est pas français. The doctor who **did** his **operation** is not French.
- ➤ Quand va-t-on **opérer** votre grand-mère? When are they going **to do** your grandmother's **operation**?

ORDONNER - S'ORDONNER

1 - To arrange, to sort out, to organize

- ➤ Les fiches **sont ordonnées** alphabétiquement. The cards **are arranged** alphabetically.
- ➤ Elle n'arrivait pas à **ordonner** ses pensées. She couldn't **sort out/organize** her thoughts.
- ➤ Pour une fois nous **avions** bien **ordonné** notre journée. For once we **had organized** our day properly.
- ➤ Il suffit de **nous ordonner** à l'avance. All we need to do is **organize ourselves** in advance.

2 - To order, to instruct

- ➤ Elle leur **a ordonné** de s'arrêter. She **ordered** them to stop.
- ➤ Ils ne peuvent pas nous **ordonner** de partir. They can't **order** us to leave.
- ➤ Qui vous **avait ordonné** de commencer? Who **had ordered/had instructed** you to start?
- ➤ Je lui **ordonnerai** de ne rien dire. I **will instruct** him/her not to say anything.

3 - To prescribe (treatment/medicine).

4 - To ordain (priest).

PARCOURIR

1 - To travel, to go all over, to cover (distance)

- ➤ Nous avons l'intention de **parcourir** cette région l'automne prochain. We intend **to travel/to go all over** this area next autumn.
- ➤ Ils vont **parcourir** toute la ville s'il le faut. They **will go all over** the town if they have to.
- ➤ Ça me plairait énormément de **parcourir** le pays de la Loire. I would really enjoy **travelling/going all over** the Pays de la Loire.
- ➤ Ils **avaient parcouru** plus de deux cents kilomètres. They **had travelled/covered** more than two hundred kilometres.

2 - To glance at, to skim through

- ➤ Elle **a parcouru** le premier rang des yeux. She **glanced at** the first row.
- ➤ J'**ai** seulement **parcouru** le journal. I **have** only **skimmed through** the newspaper.
- ➤ Elle **avait parcouru** la lettre avant de quitter la maison. She **had glanced at/skimmed through** the letter before leaving the house.
- ➤ Il vous faut aussi **parcourir** ces trois pages. You also must **glance at/skim through** these three pages.

PASSER - SE PASSER

1 - To pass, to go past, to cross

> ➤ Nous nous arrêterons quand on **aura passé** Lyon. We will stop when we **have passed/have gone past** Lyon.
> ➤ Après avoir **passé** la pharmacie vous tournez à gauche. Once you have **passed/gone past** the chemist shop turn left.
> ➤ Il comptait les voitures qui **passaient**. He used to count the cars that **were going past**.
> ➤ Quand va-t-on **passer** la frontière? When are we going **to cross** the border?

2 - To call in, to call by, to drop in, to drop by

> ➤ Il ne peut pas **passer** cet après-midi comme promis. He can't **call in/drop in** this afternoon as promised.
> ➤ Et si nous **passions** avant le dîner? What if we were **to call in/drop in** before dinner?
> ➤ Je **passerai** au pressing avant de rentrer. I **will call in** at the drycleaner's after work.
> ➤ Quand pourrais-tu **passer**? When could you **call in/drop in**?

3 - To go

> Le car **passe** sous le pont. The coach **does go** under the bridge.
> Est-ce que je peux **passer** maintenant? Can I **go** (through) now?
> Elle ne voulait pas que nous **passions** par là. She didn't want us **to go** that way.
> Il **est passé** d'un sujet à l'autre. He **went** from one subject to another.
>

4 - To spend (time)

> Nous **passerons** deux semaines à Marseille. We **will spend** two weeks in Marseille.
> Elle a de la chance de pouvoir **passer** toute la journée dans son jardin. She is lucky that she can **spend** the whole day in her garden.
> Où vont-ils **passer** le jour férié? Where are they going **to spend** the bank holiday?
> Vous **passiez** vos dimanches chez vos grands-parents? **Did** you **use to spend** your Sundays at your grandparents' house?

5 - To take (exams)

> Je n'**ai** pas encore **passé** mon permis de conduire. I **have** not **taken** my driving licence yet.

> Quand doit-il **passer** le concours? When is he due **to take** the entrance exam?

> Elle **passera** son bac le mois prochain. She **will take** her A levels next month.

> Vous **avez passé** combien d'examens? How many exams **did** you **take**?

6 - To happen, to take place

> Que va-t-il **se passer** à présent? What is going **to happen** now?

> Le vide-grenier **se passera** dans le parking derrière la gare. The car boot sale **will take place** in the car park behind the station.

> Où est-ce que cela **se passe** normalement? Where does it normally **take place**?

> Ça **s'est passé** la semaine dernière. It **happened/took place** last week.

7 - To go without, to cope without

> Je ne peux pas **me passer** d'elle. I can't **cope without** her.

> Nous **nous passerons** de sucre, c'est pas grave. We **will go without sugar**, it's not a problem.
> Ça **se passe** d'explication. It **goes without** saying.
> Ils **se passent** de tout le confort? They **cope without** all the home comforts?

8 - To pass (over), to give, to let have

> **Passe**-moi le sel s'il te plaît. Can you **pass** me the salt please?
> Tu veux qu'elle te **passe** quelque chose? Do you want her **to pass** something **over** to you?
> Je lui **passerai** le stylo dans une seconde. I'll **give** him/her the biro in a second.
> Pourriez-vous nous **passer** le document dès que vous l'aurez lu? Could you **let** us **have** the document as soon as you have read it?

9 - To be accepted (joke, proposition, request).

10 - To become, to be appointed (job description).

11 - To be showing, to be on (cinema, theatre, television, radio).

12 - To fade (colour).

13 - To be over.

14 - To strain (liquid).

PLACER - SE PLACER

1 - To place, to put

➢ **Placez** vos chaussures sous l'escalier. **Place/put** your shoes under the stairs.

➢ Il ne faut rien **placer** sur cette table basse. You mustn't **place/put** anything on this coffee table.

➢ J'**avais placé** le ticket dans mon porte-monnaie. I **had put** the ticket in my purse.

➢ Vous les **avez placés** dans une situation difficile. You **have placed/have put** them in a difficult situation.

2 - To set, to arrange

➢ Nous **placions** les serviettes comme ceci. We **used to set/used to arrange** the napkins like this.

➢ Comment **avaient**-ils **placé** les bancs? How **had** they **arranged** the benches?

➢ Où **placerons**-nous les gerbes? Where **will** we **set** the bouquets?

➢ Les coussins **sont** mal **placés**. The cushions **are** not **arranged** very well.

3 - To find a job, to find a place, to get a place

- ➤ Ils espèrent **placer** l'amie de leur fille dans la compagnie familiale. They hope **to find a job** for their daughter's friend in the family business.
- ➤ Elle essayera de **placer** sa mère dans la maison de retraite du quartier. She will try and **find** her mother **a place** in the local old people's home.
- ➤ Mon neveu n'a pas pu **placer** son fils dans son ancien collège. My nephew wasn't able **to get** his son **a place** in his former school.
- ➤ Ils **ont placé** tous les chiots. They **have found a place** (home) for all the puppies.

4 - To invest, to save

- ➤ Ils **avaient placé** toutes leurs économies dans cette initiative. They **had invested** all their savings in this business enterprise.
- ➤ Nous **plaçons** de l'argent régulièrement pour notre retraite. We **invest/save** some money regularly for our retirement.
- ➤ Quelle somme voulez-vous **placer** avec la Caisse d'Épargne? How much do you want **to invest** in the Caisse d'Épargne?
- ➤ Quand commenceras-tu à **placer** de l'argent. When will you start **to save** money?

PLAINDRE - SE PLAINDRE

1 - To complain, to moan

- ➢ J'écris pour **me plaindre** au sujet du service dans votre hôtel. I am writing **to complain** about the service in your hotel.
- ➢ Nous **nous sommes plaints** sans hésiter. We promptly **complained**.
- ➢ Trois personnes **se sont plaintes** aujourdh'ui. Three people **have complained** today.
- ➢ Arrête de **te plaindre**. Stop **complaining/moaning**.

2 - To feel sorry for, to pity, to sympathize with

- ➢ Je ne veux surtout pas qu'on **me plaigne**. Above all I don't want people **to feel sorry for** me.
- ➢ Vous la **plaignez**? **Do** you **feel sorry for her**?
- ➢ Elle les **plaint**. She **pities** them.
- ➢ Il **plaignait** son ami. He **used to sympathize with** his friend.

PLANTER - SE PLANTER

1 - To plant

- ➢ Je **planterais** beaucoup de fleurs si j'avais le temps. I **would plant** a lot of flowers if I had the time.
- ➢ Qu'est-ce que tu **planteras** ici? What **will** you **plant** here?
- ➢ Il **a planté** un petit arbre. He **planted** a little tree.
- ➢ Nous aurions dû **planter** les bulbes il y a un mois. We should have **planted** the bulbs a month ago.

2 - To hammer in, to drive in, to put, to stick

- ➢ Il est assez difficile de **planter** des clous dans ce bois. It is quite difficult **to hammer in/to drive in** some nails in this wood.
- ➢ Ils vont **planter** le poteau pour la corde à linge où? Where are they going **to drive in/to put** the post for the washing line?
- ➢ Son chaton m'**a planté** ses griffes dans le bras. His/her kitten **stuck** his claws in my arm.
- ➢ Ne **te plantes** pas devant l'écran. Don't **stick yourself** in front of the screen.

3 - To leave, to dump, to ditch

> Ils **avaient planté** leurs valises au milieu de notre séjour. They **had left/had dumped** their suitcases in the middle of our lounge.
> Il avait décidé de **planter** son travail. He had decided **to leave** his job.
> Tu ne vas tout de même pas nous **planter** là! You can't possibly **leave/dump** us here.
> C'est la troisième fois qu'elle le **plante**. She **has left/has dumped/has ditched** him for the third time.

4 - To fail, to miscalculate, to get it wrong

> Nous **nous étions plantés** dans nos prévisions. We **had failed** in our prediction.
> Malheureusement il **s'est** encore **planté**. Unfortunately he **failed/miscalculated/got it wrong** again.
> J'ai trop peur de **me planter**. I am too worried about **failing/getting it wrong**.
> Tu risques de **te planter**. You might **fail/get it wrong**.

PORTER - SE PORTER

1 - To carry

- ➢ Nous pourrions **porter** les paniers. We could **carry** the baskets.
- ➢ **J'ai porté** mon frère et ma sœur à tour de rôle. I **carried** my brother and my sister in turn.
- ➢ Qui **avait porté** les sacs dans le garage? Who **had carried** the bags in the garage?
- ➢ Elle ne veut rien **porter**. She doesn't want **to carry** anything.

2 - To endure, to bear, to have (problems/worries or affection)

- ➢ Vous **avez porté** tous ces malheurs sur vos épaules trop longtemps. You **have endured/have had** all these problems for too long.
- ➢ Il ne faut plus **porter** tous ces soucis tout seul. You don't have **to endure/to bear** all this worry on your own any more.
- ➢ C'est une croix à **porter**. It is a cross you have **to bear**.
- ➢ Il lui **porte** beaucoup d'affection. He **has** a lot of affection for him/her.

3 - To bear, to bring (produce)

> Il y a une branche du pommier qui **porte** au moins vingt fruits. There is one branch of the apple tree that **bears** at least twenty apples.
> Espérons que ça finira un jour par **porter** ses fruits. Let's hope that one day it **will bear** fruit at long last.
> Cela **a porté** le nombre de morts à dix-sept. That **brought** the number of fatalities to seventeen.
> Voilà ce qui m'**a porté** bonheur. That's what **brought** me luck.

4 - To take, to bring

> **Porte** les tasses dehors. **Take** the cups outside.
> Où veut-elle que je **porte** les magazines? Where does she want me **to take** the magazines?
> Vous pouvez **porter** les bouteilles dans la véranda. You can **take/bring** the bottles to the conservatory.
> Que faut-il **porter**? What do we have **to take/to bring**?

5 - To wear

> Il **portait** le même costume. He **was wearing** the same suit.

➤ Tu **portes** des lunettes depuis quand? How long **have** you **been wearing** glasses for?

➤ Ça **se portait** quand j'étais jeune mais plus maintenant. People **used to wear** that when I was young but they don't any more.

➤ Qu'est-ce que vous allez **porter** ce soir? What are you going **to wear** tonight?

6 - To focus, to concentrate

➤ Votre attention devrait **se porter** sur ce dernier point. You want **to focus/to concentrate** on this last point.

➤ La discussion **a** encore une fois surtout **porté** sur le problème des sans-abri. Once again the conversation mostly **focused/concentrated** on the plight of the homeless.

➤ Sur quoi est-ce que tu préfèrerais que cet entretien **porte**? What would you rather this discussion **focused/concentrated** on?

➤ Il **a** alors **porté** son regard sur lui. Then his eyes **focused** on him.

7 - To enter (name).

8 - To report (money).

9 - To be (well/unwell): reflexive form.

POSER - SE POSER

1 - To put down, to rest

> J'ai oublié où **j'ai posé** mes gants. I have forgotten where I **have put** my gloves **down**.
> Où **as**-tu **posé** les cartes postales? Where **did** you **put (down)** the postcards?
> **A**-t-il **posé** sa candidature oui ou non? **Did** he **put down** his candidature or not?
> Ne **posez** pas votre parapluie mouillé contre le mur. Don't **rest** your wet umbrella against the wall.

2 - To ask, to raise

> Il m'**a posé** une devinette. He **asked** me a puzzle.
> Vous aurez tous le temps de **poser** des questions à la fin. You will all have time **to ask/to raise** questions at the end.
> Il leur **avait posé** un nombre de questions. He **had asked/had raised** a number of questions.
> Le problème que vous nous **posez** n'est pas la fin du monde. The difficulty you **raise** is not the end of the world.

3 - To arise, to crop up, to create

> ➢ D'autres questions **se sont** tout de suite **posées**. Other questions immediately **arose**.
> ➢ Sa décision **posera** sans doute des complications. Some complications **will** most probably **crop up** because of his/her decision.
> ➢ Cela **poserait** des obstacles supplémentaires? **Would** that **create** extra obstacles?
> ➢ Ça pourrait **poser** des ennuis. Snags might **arise** as a result.

4 - To install, to put up, to lay, to fit

> ➢ L'évier n'**est** pas encore **posé** dans le cellier. The sink **has** not **been installed** in the utility room yet.
> ➢ Voici les rideaux que je vais **poser** dans la chambre d'ami. These are the curtains that I am going **to put up** in the spare bedroom.
> ➢ La moquette **sera posée** après-demain. The carpet **will be fitted/will be laid** the day after tomorrow.
> ➢ Il veut y **poser** une serrure. He wants **to fit** a lock there.

5 - To pose (art, photography).

6 - To act, to play (a role), to pretend to be.

7 - To land (bird, plane): reflexive form.

POURSUIVRE - SE POURSUIVRE

1 - To chase, to pursue

- ➤ On a vu un homme qui **poursuivait** deux adolescents. We saw one man who **was chasing** two teenagers.
- ➤ La police les **a poursuivis** jusqu'à l'église. The police **chased/pursued** them as far as the church.
- ➤ Mon chien adore **poursuivre** les écureuils. My dog loves **chasing** squirrels.
- ➤ Il m'**a poursuivi** pendant une demi-heure. He **chased** me for half an hour.

2 - To haunt, to preoccupy

- ➤ Ça m'**a poursuivi** des années. It **haunted** me for years.
- ➤ Cette image la **poursuivra** longtemps. This mental picture **will haunt** her for a long time.
- ➤ Ce souvenir d'enfance le **poursuit**? **Does** this childhood memory **haunt** him?
- ➤ Le même souci continue de les **poursuivre**. The same worry continues **to preoccupy** them.

3 - To seek, to pursue, to strive towards

- ➢ Il **poursuit** la fortune depuis toujours. He **has** always **sought** fortune.
- ➢ Il ne faut **poursuivre** que la vérité. We must **seek/pursue** only the truth.
- ➢ Elle **avait poursuivi** la gloire en vain. She **had sought/had pursued** fame in vain.
- ➢ Je vais **poursuivre** mon but jusqu'au bout. I am going **to strive towards/to pursue** my goal to the end.

4 - To continue

- ➢ Elle **poursuivra** ses études à l'étranger. She **will continue** her studies abroad.
- ➢ Est-ce que l'enquête **se poursuit**? **Is** the investigation **continuing**?
- ➢ Les recherches **s'étaient poursuivies** jusqu'à l'aube. The search **had continued** until dawn.
- ➢ **Poursuivez** je vous en prie. Please **continue**.

5 - To prosecute

- ➢ Ils **seront poursuivis** en justice tous les deux. Both of them **will be prosecuted**.

> ➤ J'**ai été poursuivi** pour excès de vitesse. I **was prosecuted** for speeding.
> ➤ Il est possible d'**être poursuivi** pour moins que ça. It is possible **to be prosecuted** for less than that.
> ➤ C'est lui qui **a été poursuivi** en justice pour le cambriolage? Is it him who **was prosecuted** for the burglary?

POUSSER - SE POUSSER

1 - To push, to move out of the way

> ➤ Ma petite-fille veut **pousser** le chariot dans les supermarchés. My granddaughter wants **to push** the trolley in supermarkets.
> ➤ Nous **pousserons** les fauteuils pour avoir plus de place. We'**ll push** the armchairs so that we have more room.
> ➤ Ils **se sont poussés** pour laisser passer le vélo. They **moved out of the way** so that the bike could go through.
> ➤ Vous pourriez **pousser** vos bagages par hasard? Could you **move** your luggage **out of the way** at all?

2 - To urge, to drive on, to go too far

> Qu'est-ce qui vous **a poussé** à faire ça? What **urged** you to do that?
> Elle **a** trop **poussé** ses enfants à l'école primaire. She **drove** her children **on** too much when they were at primary school.
> Il a le chic pour **pousser** la plaisanterie trop loin. He always **goes too far** with his jokes.
> Il s'agit de savoir quand s'arrêter de **pousser**. What we have to do is stop before we **go too far**.

3 - To continue, to carry on, to pursue

> Je voudrais **pousser** notre débat après le repas. I would like **to continue/to pursue** our argument after the meal.
> Il nous faudra **pousser** les négociations sans lui. We will have **to continue** to negotiate without him.
> Les pourparlers n'avaient pas pu **être poussés**. It had not been possible **to continue/to pursue** the talk.
> C'est un thème à **pousser** une autre fois. This is an issue **to be continued/to be pursued** another time.

4 - To let out, to utter, to shout, to scream

> Quelqu'un **avait poussé** un cri effrayant. Someone **had let out** a terrifying shriek.

> ➢ J'ai **poussé** un long soupir. I **let out** a long sigh.
> ➢ Le pauvre animal **poussait** d'étranges sons. The poor animal **was letting out** weird sounds.
> ➢ Elle **a poussé** une plainte. She **let out** a moan.

5 - To grow

> ➢ Beaucoup de jonquilles **poussent** dans la plate-bande. A lot of daffodils **grow** in the flowerbed.
> ➢ L'arbre **avait poussé** de dix centimètres environ. The tree **had grown** about ten centimetres.
> ➢ Quand est-ce que votre garçon va s'arrêter de **pousser**! When is your boy going to stop **growing**!
> ➢ Tes cheveux **poussent** vite n'est-ce pas? Your hair **grows** fast doesn't it?

PRENDRE - SE PRENDRE

1 - To take

> ➢ Je vais **prendre** mes lunettes de soleil. I am going **to take** my sunglasses.
> ➢ Elle n'a pas besoin de **prendre** de l'argent. She doesn't need **to take** some money.
> ➢ Vous **avez pris** ça comme un compliment? **Did** you **take** that as a compliment?

> ➤ On **prendra** le métro. We **will take** the tube.

2 - To buy, to get

> ➤ J'**ai pris** des croissants à la boulangerie. I **got/bought** some croissants at the bread shop.
> ➤ Tu pourrais me **prendre** le journal? Could you **get/buy** the newspaper for me?
> ➤ Il faut **prendre** de l'essence. We must **get/buy** some petrol.
> ➤ Qu'est-ce qu'elle **avait pris** à la boucherie? What had she **got/bought** at the butcher's shop?

3 - To have (to eat or to drink)

> ➤ A quelle heure est-ce que vous **prenez** le petit-déjeuner d'habitude? At what time **do** you usually **have** breakfast?
> ➤ Comme dessert nous **prendrons** des glaces à la praline. We **will have** praline ice cream for dessert.
> ➤ Il faut **prendre** quelque chose. You must **have** something (to eat or drink).
> ➤ Ils vont **prendre** l'apéritif sur la terrasse. They are going **to have** an aperitif on the patio.

4 - To catch, to trap: reflexive form.

5 - To hit (emotions, sensations).

6 - To charge (money).

PRESSER - SE PRESSER

1 - To squeeze, to press

> ➢ **Pressez** un peu de citron dessus. **Squeeze** a little lemon on it.
> ➢ Elle m'**a pressé** dans ses bras. She **squeezed** me in her arms.
> ➢ Tout va se froisser si c'**est pressé** comme ça.
> Everything is going to get creased if it **is squeezed** like that.
> ➢ Le raisin **a été pressé** hier. The grapes **were pressed** yesterday.

2 - To push, to press

> ➢ **Presse** le bouton une deuxième fois. **Push/press** the switch a second time.
> ➢ Qu'est-ce qu'on **presse**? What **do** we **push/press**?
> ➢ Elle va casser la sonnette si elle la **presse** comme ça. She is going to break the doorbell if she **pushes/presses** it like this.
> ➢ Je ne vois pas ce qu'il faut **presser** pour mettre le chauffage en marche. I can't see what I have **to push/to press** to switch the central heating on.

3 - To hurry

> **Pressez-vous** on va manquer le bateau. **Hurry up** we are going to miss the boat.
> Elle l'**a** trop **pressé**. She **hurried** him too much.
> Il faudra que vous **vous pressiez**. You will have **to hurry up**.
> Ils **étaient pressés**. They **were in a hurry**.

4 - To press (clothes).

5 - To urge.

RAPPELER - SE RAPPELER

1 - To call back

> Ils nous **avaient rappelés**. They **had called** us back.
> Je **rappellerai** ce soir. I **will call back** tonight.
> Il **a rappelé** le docteur. He **called back** the doctor.
> Qui **rappelleriez**-vous? Who **would** you **call back**?

2 - To remind

- ➤ Je vous **rappelle** qu'il est défendu de fumer. I **remind** you that it is forbidden to smoke.
- ➤ Il nous **rappelait** notre père. He **used to remind** us of our father.
- ➤ Vous leur **avez rappelé** les règles? **Did** you **remind** them what the rules are?
- ➤ **Rappelez**-nous à nos anciens voisins. **Do remind** us to our old (former) neighbours.

3 - To remember

- ➤ Elle ne **se rappelle** jamais de moi. She never remembers me.
- ➤ Tu ne te **rappelles** pas? You can't **remember**?
- ➤ Après ça il **s'est rappelé**. After that he **did remember**.
- ➤ Essayez de **vous rappeler** le numéro. Try and **remember** the number.

RAPPORTER - SE RAPPORTER

1 - To bring back

> ➢ Elle lui **avait rapporté** un beau souvenir de ses vacances. She **had brought back** a lovely souvenir from her holiday for him/her.
> ➢ Qu'est-ce que tu nous **as rapporté**? What **have** you **brought back** for us?
> ➢ Nous **rapporterons** la tondeuse demain. We **will bring back** the mower tomorrow.
> ➢ Elle n'**a** pas **rapporté** mes disques. She **did** not **bring** my disks **back**.

2 - To produce, to bring in

> ➢ Son jardin potager **avait rapporté** pas mal de légumes malgré le temps. His market garden **had produced** a fair amount of vegetables despite the weather.
> ➢ Ce placement vous **a**-t-il **rapporté**? **Did** this investment **produce** a profit?
> ➢ Ça **rapporterait** combien vous pensez? How much do you think that it **would bring in**?
> ➢ Mes actions **rapportent** assez d'argent. My shares **bring in** enough money.

3 - To concern, to relate, to express

- ➢ Ça ne **se rapporte** plus à cela. It **does** not **concern** that any more.
- ➢ Est-ce que votre question **se rapporte** au sujet actuel? Does your question **relate** to/**concern** the present point?
- ➢ A quoi **se rapporte** cette remarque? What **does** this remark **relate** to?
- ➢ Cela **se rapporte** justement à ce que je pensais. Funnily enough that **does express** what I was thinking.

4 - To tell, to report, to describe

- ➢ Je te **rapporte** exactement ce qu'on m'a dit. I **am telling** you what I have been told word for word.
- ➢ Il nous **avait rapporté** qu'elle allait mieux. He **had told** us that she was better.
- ➢ Le déroulement du projet **sera rapporté** par qui? Who **will report/will describe** the project from beginning to end?
- ➢ Ce qu'elle vous **a rapporté** n'est pas facile à croire. What she **has described** to you is not easy to believe.

5 - To tell tales (on people).

RATTRAPER - SE RATTRAPER

1 - To catch (up), to recapture

- ➢ On ne la **rattrapera** pas une deuxième fois elle a compris. She **will** not **get caught** a second time no way.
- ➢ Nous vous **rattraperons** dans quelques minutes. We **will catch** you **up** in a few minutes.
- ➢ Je **me suis rattrapé** à lui quand j'ai glissé. I **caught myself** on him when I slipped.
- ➢ Les deux personnes **ont été rattrapées** à Nice. The two people **have been recaptured** in Nice.

2 - To save, to salvage, to put right, to make up for

- ➢ Nous verrons s'il est possible de **rattraper** quoi que ce soit de l'inondation dans la cave. We shall have to see whether anything can be **saved/salvaged** in the flooded cellar.
- ➢ C'était trop tard pour **rattraper** mon erreur. It was too late for me **to put right** my mistake.
- ➢ Ils ont l'intention d'essayer de **rattraper** leur oubli. They do intend to try **to make up for** their slip-up.
- ➢ Est-ce qu'elle **a rattrapé** son retard? **Did** she **make up** for being late?

3 - To recoup, to recover, to catch up, to get up to date

➤ Le temps perdu ne **se rattrape** jamais. You can never **recoup** wasted time.

➤ Est-ce que vous pensiez pouvoir **rattraper** ce déficit? Did you feel that you would be able **to recoup/to recover** this deficit?

➤ Il fait le maximum pour **se rattraper** dans ses études depuis qu'il est guéri. He has been doing all he can **to catch up/to get up to date** in his studies since he has been well again.

➤ J'ai mis longtemps à **me rattraper** après ma longue absence au bureau. It took me a long time **to recover/to catch up/to get up to date** after my long absence from the office.

RECUEILLIR - SE RECUEILLIR

1 - To gather, to collect, to get

➤ Elle **recueillera** tous les questionnaires elle-même. She **will gather/will collect/will get** all the questionnaires herself.

- Nous **avons** maintenant **recueilli** toutes les demandes d'emploi. We **have gathered/have collected/have got** all the job applications now.
- Il devrait **recueillir** le plus de voix. He should **get** the most votes.
- Ils **recueilleront** enfin le fruit de leur travail. At last they **will get** the fruit of their labour.

2 - To record

- J'**avais recueilli** tous les renseignements nécessaires. I **had recorded** all the necessary information.
- Quand allez-vous **recueillir** toutes les réponses? When are you going **to record** all the replies?
- Il faut **recueillir** la liste des hôtels à deux étoiles de la ville. We need **to record** the list of the two-star hotels in the town.
- Pas besoin de **recueillir** tous ces détails. There is no need **to record** all these particulars.

3 - To welcome, to receive, to take in (usually people/animals who are in temporary difficulties)

- On les **recueillerait** volontiers chez nous si nous avions la place. We **would welcome/would receive** them in our home quite happily if we had the room.
- Ils ne pouvaient pas **recueillir** les deux chiens eux-mêmes. They couldn't **take in** the two dogs themselves.

➢ Une gentille voisine **avait recueilli** la fillette en larmes chez elle. A nice neighbour **had taken in** the little girl in tears.

➢ Qui **recueillera** les sinistrés de l'explosion en attendant? Who **will take in** the bomb victims in the meantime?

4 - To gather one's thoughts, to meditate, to reflect

➢ J'ai vu le couple âgé **se recueillir** sur sa tombe. I saw the old couple **gathering theirs thoughts** in front of his/her grave.

➢ Elle **se recueille** dans cette chapelle régulièrement. She **meditates** in this chapel regularly.

➢ Il est bon de **se recueillir** de temps en temps. It is a good thing **to gather one's thoughts/to meditate/to reflect** from time to time.

➢ Il aime **se recueillir** devant la photo de sa femme avant de se coucher. He likes **to reflect** looking at his wife's photo before going to bed.

RÉCUPÉRER

1 - To recover, to get well

> ➤ Elle **récupère** petit à petit. She **is** gradually **recovering**.
> ➤ Plusieurs joggeurs **récupéraient** sur un banc. Several joggers **were recovering** on a bench.
> ➤ Il faut surtout de la patience quand on **récupère** après une opération. Above all you need patience when you **are recovering** from an operation.
> ➤ Il va là-bas dans le but de **récupérer** (sa santé). He is going over there in order **to get well** again.

2 - To get (people or things back)

> ➤ Tu peux venir **récupérer** tes enfants à huit heures? Can you come **to get** your children at eight?
> ➤ Je vais **récupérer** mes affaires. I am going **to get** my things **back**.
> ➤ Nous **récupèrerons** les hamsters le cinq septembre. We **will get** the hamsters **back** on the fifth of September.
> ➤ **Ont**-ils **récupéré** leur caméscope? **Have** they **got back** their camcorder?

3 - To salvage, to rescue

> ➤ Il n'y avait rien à **récupérer** de passable pour le vide-grenier. There was nothing worth **salvaging** for the car boot sale.
> ➤ J'**ai récupéré** assez de tissu dans un vieux drap pour faire une taie d'oreiller. I **have salvaged** enough material out of an old sheet to make one pillowcase.
> ➤ Qu'as-tu pu **récupérer**? What have you been able **to salvage/to rescue**?
> ➤ Tout ce qu'elles **ont récupéré** est dans le garage. Everything that they **have salvaged/have rescued** is in the garage.

4 - To make up (time)

> ➤ J'ai promis à mon patron que je **récupèrerai** le temps perdu pendant le week-end. I promised my boss that I **would make up** for loss time during the weekend.
> ➤ Vous **récupèrerez** demain sans faute. You **will make** it **up** tomorrow without fail.
> ➤ Quand pourra-t-il **récupérer** toutes ces heures? When will he be able **to make up** all these hours?
> ➤ Il n'y a pas eu moyen de **récupérer** le temps perdu après l'interruption. There was no way we could **make up** the time lost because of the interruption.

REGARDER - SE REGARDER

1 - To look, to watch

- ➤ Vous **avez regardé** la jolie vue? **Did** you **look** at the beautiful scenery?
- ➤ Elle aurait dû **regarder**. She should have **looked/watched**.
- ➤ Ils **regardent** beaucoup de feuilletons. They **watch** a lot of soap operas.
- ➤ On **regardait** les oiseaux faire leurs nids. We **used to watch** the birds nesting.

2 - To consider, to see, to think carefully

- ➤ Je les **ai** toujours **regardés** comme de la famille. I **have** always **considered** them as relations of mine.
- ➤ Il **regarde** ça comme un reproche. He **sees** that as a criticism.
- ➤ Ils la **regardaient** comme une ennemie. They **used to see** her as an enemy.
- ➤ **Regarde** bien avant d'accepter. **Think carefully** before you accept.

3 - To concern, to be one's business, to involve, to affect

- ➢ Cette affaire ne les **regarde** pas du tout. This business **does** not **involve/affect** them at all.
- ➢ Je pense que ça me **regarde**. I do think that it **involves/affects** me.
- ➢ Est-ce que cela les **regarde**? **Is** it any of **their business**?
- ➢ Notre situation ne les **regardait** plus. Our situation **was** no longer any of **their business**.

RÉGLER

1 - To pay, to settle

- ➢ Il faudra **régler** la facture avant la fin du mois. We will have **to pay/to settle** the invoice before the end of the month.
- ➢ Je vous **règle** ça tout de suite. **I'll pay** you for that straight away.
- ➢ Vous **règlerez** la note avant de partir. You **will pay/will settle** the bill before leaving.
- ➢ Il ne peut pas **régler** ses dettes. He can't **pay** his debts.

2 - To adjust, to match

- ➤ Il **a** déjà **réglé** le chauffage central? **Has** he already **adjusted** the central heating?
- ➤ **Règle** ta montre sur l'heure française. **Adjust** your watch to French time.
- ➤ Je ne sais pas **régler** le mécanisme de cette machine. I don't know how **to adjust** the mechanism of this appliance.
- ➤ Elle essaie de **régler** sa vie sur celle de sa sœur jumelle. She tries **to match** her life to her twin sister's.

3 - To fix, to settle, to sort out

- ➤ L'emploi du temps **a été réglé** par qui? Who **fixed** the timetable?
- ➤ L'affaire **avait été réglée** sans trop de problèmes. The situation **had been settled out/had been sorted out** without too many difficulties.
- ➤ Quand **règleront**-ils leur différend? When **will** they **sort out** their differences?
- ➤ Il y a quelque chose qu'elle veut **régler** avec son patron. There is something she wants **to sort out** with her boss.

REJETER - SE REJETER

1 - To throw back/up

> Elle **a** gentiment **rejeté** notre ballon par-dessus la clôture. She kindly **threw back** our ball over the fence.
> Quand nous allions à la pêche mon grand-père **rejetait** toujours les poissons à la mer. When we used to go fishing my grandfather always **used to throw back** the fish in the sea.
> La traversée était si mauvaise que j'**ai rejeté** tout mon petit-déjeuner. The crossing was so bad that I **threw up** my whole breakfast.
> Il vaut mieux que je ne te dise pas ce que la chienne vient de **rejeter**. It is better if I don't tell you what the dog has just **thrown up**.

2 - To reject, to dismiss, to turn down

> Pourquoi est-ce que vous **rejetez** ma proposition? Why **do** you **reject** my proposal?
> Son idée **sera** sans doute **rejetée** par tout le monde. No doubt his/her idea **will be rejected/will be dismissed/will be turned down** by everybody.
> Il **a rejeté** mon offre. He **rejected/turned down** my offer.

> Ils **ont rejeté** son initiative. They **have rejected/have dismissed/have turned down** his/her plan.

3 - To shift, to transfer

> Ils **ont** encore une fois **rejeté** la responsabilité sur nous. Once again they **shifted** the responsibility onto us.
> Vous n'allez tout de même pas **rejeter** le blâme sur eux! You can't possibly **shift** the blame on them.
> Elle **avait rejeté** la faute sur son ami. She **had shifted** the fault on her friend.
> Ne **rejetez** pas la culpabilité sur moi. **Do** not **shift** the guilt onto me.

4 - To fall back

> Encore une fois il a fallu que je **me rejette** sur mes beaux-parents. Once again I had **to fall back** on my in-laws.
> Ça ne les a pas du tout dérangés qu'elle **se rejette** sur eux. They didn't mind at all that she **fell back** on them.
> S'il n'y a plus de vin on **se rejettera** sur la bière. If there is no wine left **we'll fall back** on the beer.
> On avait encore faim alors nous **nous sommes rejetés** sur le plateau de fromage. We were still hungry so **we fell back** on the cheese board.

RELEVER - SE RELEVER

1 - To stand up, to get up

- Ce n'est pas la peine de **vous relever**. Don't bother **to stand up/to get up**.
- Je **me suis relevé** tout de suite. I **stood up/got up** straight away.
- Des chaises sont tombées dans le vent pourriez-vous les **relever** s'il vous plaît? Some chairs have fallen down in the wind could you **stand** them **up** (again) please?
- Les photos sont tombées je vais les **relever**. The photos have fallen down I am going **to stand** them **up** again.

2 - To go up, to pull up, to put up, to lift up, to raise

- Ta jupe **relève** sur le côté droit. Your dress **goes up** on the right side.
- **Relève** tes chaussettes. **Pull up** your socks.
- Je préfèrerais qu'on **relève** le tableau de un ou deux centimètres. I would rather the picture **was put up/raised** one or two centimetres.
- Elle **a relevé** la tête. She lifted up her head.

3 - To improve, to enhance

> Le but est de **relever** le niveau de vie des personnes moins aisées. The aim is **to improve** the living standard of people who are less well off.
> Qu'est-ce qui pourrait **relever** l'économie d'après toi? What could **improve** the economy in your opinion?
> La couleur de ton chemisier **relève** ton teint. The colour of your blouse **enhances** your complexion.
> Le citron **relève** le goût du poisson. Lemon **improves/enhances** the taste of fish.

4 - To take over

> Il la **relèvera** à deux heures. He **will take over** from her at two.
> À quelle heure **a-t-il été relevé**? At what time **did** they **take over** from him?
> Qui me **relèvera**? Who **will take over** from me?
> Voulez-vous qu'on vous **relève**? Do you want someone **to take over** from you?

5 - To notice

> J'**ai relevé** son hésitation. I **did notice** his/her dithering.
> **Avez**-vous **relevé** leur gêne? **Did** you **notice** their embarrassment?

> ➢ Je n'**avais** rien **relevé** de bizarre. I **had** not **noticed** anything strange.
> ➢ Son retard **a été relevé**. His lateness **was noticed**.

6 - To write down, to take down

> ➢ Pourquoi voulez-vous **relever** mon nom? Why do you want **to write down/to take down** my name?
> ➢ Qui **relèvera** les numéros? Who **will write down/will take down** the numbers?
> ➢ Je dois **relever** vos coordonnées. I must **take down/write down** your particulars.
> ➢ Il faut **relever** le compteur du gaz. You need **to take down/to write down** the figure on the gas meter.

7 - To release, to relieve

> ➢ Elle l'**a relevé** de sa promesse. She **released** him from his promise.
> ➢ Je vous **relève** de vos responsabilités. I **release/relieve** you from your obligations.
> ➢ Quand **seront**-ils enfin **relevés** de ce devoir? When **will** they finally **be relieved** from this duty?
> ➢ On l'**avait relevé** de ses fonctions. He **had been released/had been relieved** from his functions.

8 - To recover

> ➤ Elle **s'était** à peine **relevée** de sa pneumonie. She **had** only just **recovered** from her pneumonia.
> ➤ J'espère qu'il **se relèvera** de sa maladie rapidement. I hope that he **will recover** quickly from his illness.
> ➤ Il mettra longtemps à **se relever** de son deuil. He will take a long time **to recover** from his loss.
> ➤ Il est difficile de **se relever** d'une expérience comme ça. It is difficult **to recover** from an experience like this.

9 - To be a matter for

> ➤ Ceci **relève** du service personnel. This **is a matter for** the personnel section.
> ➤ Est-ce que ça **relève** de la Chambre de Commerce? **Is** that **a matter for** the Chambre de Commerce?
> ➤ Cette affaire ne **relève** pas de la municipalité. This business **is** not **a matter for** the council.
> ➤ Cette histoire ne **relève** pas de mon bureau. This issue **is** not **a matter for** my office.

10 - To season, to bring out (the flavour)

> ➤ Le plat n'**était** pas assez **relevé**. This dish **was** not **seasoned** enough.

> Pensez-vous que je n'**ai** pas assez **relevé** la sauce? Do you think that I **have** not **seasoned** the sauce sufficiently?
> Si c'**est** trop **relevé** les gosses ne le mangent pas. If it **is** too **seasoned** the kids don't want to eat it.
> Les épices **relèvent** le goût bien sûr. Spices **bring out** the flavour of course.

11 - To rebuild, to restore, to put back on its feet.

12 - To collect (school work).

13 - To react/reply (to negative behaviour/comment).

REMETTRE - SE REMETTRE

1 - To put off, to postpone

➢ La visite **sera remise** au mois prochain. The visit **will be put off** until next month.

➢ L'interview a dû **être remise** au lendemain. The interview had **to be put off/postponed** to the next day.

➢ C'est dommage qu'il ait fallu **remettre** la fête d'anniversaire de mariage. It is a pity that we have had **to postpone** the wedding anniversary party.

➢ Pourquoi **ont**-ils **remis** leur départ? Why **did** they **postpone** their departure?

2 - To get over

➢ **Se sont**-ils **remis** de leur accident? **Have** they **got over** their accident?

➢ Elle ne **se remettra** jamais de sa surprise. She **will** never **get over** her surprise.

➢ Petit à petit il **se remet** de sa dépression avec les médicaments et surtout avec le soutien de sa famille. He **is** slowly **getting over** his depression with drugs and above all with the support of his family.

➢ Quand je **me serai remise** de mon opération on fera une escapade ensemble. As soon as **I have got over** my operation we'll go on a mini-break together.

3 - To give, to hand in

- ➢ **As**-tu **remis** la lettre au professeur? **Did** you **give** the letter to the teacher?
- ➢ Je lui **ai remis** le message. I **gave** him/her the message.
- ➢ Nous n'oublierons pas de leur **remettre** l'enveloppe. We will not forget **to give** them the enveloppe.
- ➢ Elle avait l'intention de **remettre** sa démission. She had intended **to hand in** her resignation.

4 - To make up, to get back together

- ➢ Préfèreriez-vous qu'il **se remette** avec son ancien collègue? Would you prefer that he **made up** with his former colleague?
- ➢ C'est fini je ne **me remettrai** jamais avec eux. That's the end I will never **make up** with them.
- ➢ Ils **se sont remis** ensemble il y a seulement quelques jours. They **got back together** only a few days ago.
- ➢ Peut-être qu'un jour tu **te remettras** avec lui. Maybe one day you **will get back together** with him.

5 - 'Do' again: The prefix 're-' (sometimes just 'r' before a vowel) in front of a verb in French is one of the ways to say 'verb+again' for many of the verbs. Some of the meanings in *'mettre - se mettre'* are also appropriate to use with this prefix, *'remettre - se remettre'*, and must be added to the list of meanings.

REMONTER

1 - To go back, to come back up

- ➤ Il vous faut **remonter** jusqu'au début. You will need **to go back** to the beginning.
- ➤ Tu **es remonté** dans mon estime. You **have gone back** in my estimation.
- ➤ Ça **remonte** à une vingtaine d'années. It **goes back** to about twenty years ago.
- ➤ La boîte **est remontée** à la surface du lac. The box **came back up** to the surface of the lake.

2 - To raise, to put (higher) up

- ➤ Ils vont **remonter** le mur. They are going **to raise** the wall.
- ➤ Elle **remonte** toujours le bord de son manteau. She always **puts up** the collar of her coat.
- ➤ Il a voulu qu'on **remonte** le cadre. He wanted the picture **put (higher) up**.
- ➤ Tu veux que je **remonte** le store du bureau? Do you want me **to put up** the blind in the study?

3 - To put together again

- ➢ Quand pourras-tu **remonter** la radio? When will you be able **to put** the radio **together again**?
- ➢ Impossible de **remonter** le meuble. We simply couldn't **put** the piece of furniture **together again**.
- ➢ Il était en train de **remonter** le moteur. He was in the middle of **putting** the engine **back together again**.
- ➢ Est-ce que tu sais comment **remonter** le vélo? Do you know how **to put** the bicycle **back together again**?

4 - To wind up (mechanical things)

- ➢ Elle a encore une montre qu'il faut **remonter**! She still has a watch that you have **to wind up**!
- ➢ Il sait **remonter** son jouet tout seul. He can **wind up** his toy on his own.
- ➢ C'est moi qui **remonte** la vieille horloge. I am the one who **winds up** the old grandfather clock.
- ➢ Ça **se remonte** comme ça regarde c'est simple. You **wind** it **up** like that, look it's easy!

5 - To renew, to replace (belongings), to refurnish

- ➢ Elle **remonte** sa garde-robe tous les printemps. She **renews** her wardrobe every spring.

> Ils ont mis plusieurs années pour **remonter** leur appartement après l'incendie. It took them several years **to replace things** in their flat after the fire.

> Nous n'avons pas assez d'argent pour **remonter** notre foyer. We don't have enough money **to refurnish** our home.

> N'étant pas assurés pour le cambriolage nous avons mis trois ans à **nous remonter**. As we were not insured for burglary it took us three years **to replace our furniture**.

6 - To cheer up, to set back on their feet, to rebuild

> Elle sait comment me **remonter** le moral. She knows how **to cheer** me **up**.

> Personne n'est arrivé à lui **remonter** le moral. Nobody has managed **to cheer** him/her **up**.

> Il va falloir énormément de travail pour **remonter** l'entreprise. A huge amount of work is going to be necessary in order **to set** the business **back on its feet**.

> Est-ce que ce sera trop tard pour **remonter** notre affaire? Will it be too late **to rebuild** our company?

7 - 'do' again: Also see '*monter - se monter*' for additional meanings with the prefix 're-' (verb+again), '*remonter - se remonter*'.

RENDRE - SE RENDRE

1 - To give back, to return, to repay

➢ Est-ce qu'il t'**a rendu** tes outils? **Did** he **give** your tools **back** to you?

➢ Elle a décidé de lui **rendre** la bague. She decided **to give** the ring **back** to him.

➢ Ils ne m'**ont** jamais **rendu** l'argent. They never **gave back** the money to me.

➢ Je lui **ai rendu** le compliment. I **gave back** the compliment.

2 - To make (+ adjective)

➢ C'est quelque chose qui m'a toujours **rendu** malade. That's something that **has** always **made** me sick.

➢ Peux-tu **te rendre** utile? Can you **make yourself** useful?

➢ Notre visite les **rendait** toujours très heureux. Our visit always **used to make** them very happy.

➢ Ça **rendrait** le colis trop lourd. That **would make** the parcel too heavy.

3 - To give in, to give oneself up

> ➤ Vous **vous rendez? Do** you **give in**?
> ➤ Il a dit qu'il ne **se rendra** jamais. He said that he **will** never **give in**.
> ➤ On avait préféré **se rendre**. We chose **to give up/to give ourselves up**.
> ➤ L'adolescent **s'est rendu** à la police le jour suivant. The teenager **gave himself up** to the police the following day.

4 - To face (facts, the obvious), to accept

> ➤ Il a bien fallu que nous **nous rendions** à l'évidence. We just had **to face** the facts.
> ➤ Ils ont fini par **se rendre** à l'évidence. They **faced** the facts in the end.
> ➤ Il ne veut pas **se rendre** à l'évidence. He doesn't want **to face** the obvious.
> ➤ Quand **vous rendrez**-vous à l'évidence? When **will** you **accept** the facts?

5 - To go, to get (to places)

> ➤ Comment **se rend**-il à son travail? How **does** he **go/get** to work?

> ➤ Ils **se rendront** à la mairie à midi. They **will go/will get** to the town hall at noon.
> ➤ Je peux **m'y rendre** mardi. I can **go/get** there on Tuesday.
> ➤ Nous **nous étions rendus** chez le dentiste avec un peu de retard. We **had got** to the dentist's a little late.

6 - To be sick, to vomit

> ➤ Il **a rendu** tout le matin. He **has been sick** the whole morning.
> ➤ Presque tous les passagers **rendaient** sur le ferry. Nearly all the passengers **were sick** on the ferry.
> ➤ Je crois que je vais **rendre**. I think that I am going **to be sick**.
> ➤ Qui **a rendu** dans l'escalier? Who **has been sick** in the stairs?

7 - To render, to convey.

8 - To give out/produce (noise, liquid).

RENVERSER

1 - To knock over/down

> ➢ Il **a été renversé** par une moto hier. He **was knocked over** by a motorbike yesterday.
> ➢ Qui **a renversé** le seau? Who **knocked** the bucket **over**?
> ➢ Arrête de courir tu vas **renverser** quelqu'un. Stop running you are going **to knock** somebody **down**.
> ➢ J'ai peur que cette nouvelle ne la **renverse** complètement. I am worried that this piece of news might really **knock** her **down**.

2 - To turn upside-down, to upset

> ➢ Elle **avait renversé** des cageots pour faire des tables basses de fortune. She **had turned** some crates **upside-down** to use as makeshift coffee tables.
> ➢ Il vaut mieux **renverser** les pots pour les faire sécher. It would be better **to turn** the pots **upside-down** to dry them.
> ➢ Ça **a** tout **renversé**. It **turned** everything **upside-down**.
> ➢ Ses plans **ont été renversés** à cause de toi. His/her plans **have been turned upside-down/have been upset** because of you.

3 - To spill

- ➤ Tu vas **renverser** la bière de papa. You are going **to spill** dad's beer.
- ➤ Il **renverse** toujours quelque chose. He always **spills** something.
- ➤ Qu'est-ce qui **a été renversé** sur ce tapis? What **has been spilt** on this carpet?
- ➤ J'**ai renversé** un peu de sauce sur ta jolie nappe. I **have spilt** a bit of sauce on your pretty tablecloth.

4 - To bring down (the government), to overthrow

- ➤ Ils voulaient **renverser** le gouvernement une bonne fois pour toutes. They wanted **to bring down** the government once and for all.
- ➤ Cela pourrait **renverser** le gouvernement. That could **bring down** the government.
- ➤ Ce n'est pas ça qui **renverserait** le gouvernement. That is not what **would overthrow** the government.
- ➤ Il est ridicule de penser que rien ne pourrait **renverser** le gouvernement. It is silly to think that nothing could **overthrow** the government.

5 - To reverse, to turn (things) round.

REPASSER

1 - To iron

- ➤ Il a toujours détesté **repasser**. He has always hated **ironing**.
- ➤ Quand vas-tu **repasser** tes chemises? When are you going **to iron** your shirts?
- ➤ Je **repasserais** ses affaires aussi si je ne travaillais pas. I **would** also **iron** his/her things if I didn't work.
- ➤ Vous écoutez la radio en **repassant**? You listen to the radio whilst you **iron**?

2 - 'do again': Also see '*passer - se passer*' for additional meanings with the prefix '-re' (verb+again), '*repasser*- **se repasser**'.

REPORTER - SE REPORTER

1 - To postpone, to put off, to delay

- ➢ Pourquoi est-ce que l'émission **avait** encore **été reportée**? Why **had** the programme **been postponed** once again?
- ➢ La fête **est reportée** à cause du décès du maire. The fête **is postponed** because of the death of the mayor.
- ➢ Nous **avons reporté** notre déménagement à l'année prochaine. We **have put off** moving house until next year.
- ➢ Il aurait mieux valu que vous **ayez reporté** la réunion. It would have been better **had** you **delayed** the meeting.

2 - To consult, to turn (to), to look up, to refer (to)

- ➢ **Reportez-vous** à la bibliographie. **Consult/turn** to/**look up** the bibliography.
- ➢ Nous **nous sommes reportés** au chapitre trois. We **turned** to chapter three.
- ➢ Je **me reporterai** à mes notes. I **will consult/will look up** my notes.
- ➢ **S'était**-il **reporté** à la lettre originale? **Had** he **referred** to the original letter?

3 - To think back to

- ➢ Je **me reporte** souvent à ce jour-là. I often **think back** to that day.
- ➢ C'est avec beaucoup de bonheur qu'il **se reporte** à son enfance. He **does think back** to his childhood with a lot of pleasure.
- ➢ Je **me suis reporté** au début de l'année plus d'une fois. I **have been thinking back** to the beginning of the year more than once.
- ➢ Quand nous **nous reportons** à cette soirée nous sommes très tristes. When we **think back** to that evening we feel very sad.

4 - To transfer.

5 - 'do again': Also see '*porter - se porter*' for additional meanings with the prefix 're-' (verb+again), '*reporter -se reporter*'.

REPOSER -SE REPOSER

1 - To rest

- ➤ Les chats **se reposaient** au soleil. The cats **were resting** in the sun.
- ➤ Où est-ce que vous **vous êtes reposé**? Where **did** you **rest**?
- ➤ Il ne voulait pas **se reposer**. He didn't want **to rest**.
- ➤ Elles **se reposeront** chez moi. They **will rest** at my house.

2 - To be supported, to rest

- ➤ Ça pourrait **reposer** sur les poutres. That could **be supported** by the beams.
- ➤ La planche **repose** sur deux boîtes. The board **is resting** on two boxes.
- ➤ Ne **reposez** rien là-dessus c'est trop fragile. Don't **rest** anything on this it is too fragile.
- ➤ Le gril du barbecue peut **reposer** sur des briques. The barbecue grid can **rest** on some bricks.

3 - To depend, to be based

- ➤ Votre raisonnement **repose** sur quoi exactement? Your interpretation **is based** on what exactly?
- ➤ Tout **repose** maintenant sur vos aveux. Everything **depends** on your confession now.
- ➤ Sa conclusion ne **reposait** que sur un bruit. His conclusion **was** only **based** on rumours.
- ➤ Cela **reposera** sur les résultats de l'enquête. It **will depend/will be based** on the results of the survey.

4 - To rely on

- ➤ Ne **vous reposez** surtout pas sur lui pour décider. What ever you do don't **rely** on him to decide.
- ➤ Il **s'est** toujours **reposé** sur sa femme pour la paperasserie. He **has** always **relied** on his wife for the paperwork.
- ➤ Il est grand temps de ne plus **te reposer** sur autrui. It is about time you stopped **relying** on others.
- ➤ Puis-je **me reposer** sur vous pour les formalités à accomplir? Can I **rely** on you to see to the formalities?

5 - 'Do again': Also see '*poser - se poser*' for additional meanings with the prefix 're-' (verb+again), '*reposer - se reposer*'.

REPRÉSENTER - SE REPRÉSENTER

1 - To represent

> ➤ Nous voulons **représenter** notre école. We wish **to represent** our school.
> ➤ Il **représentera** la compagnie à la conférence. He **will represent** the company at the conference.
> ➤ Qui va te **représenter**? Who is going **to represent** you?
> ➤ Personne ne voulait la **représenter**. No one wanted **to represent** her.

2 - To show, to depict, to illustrate

> ➤ Il a dit que son dessin **représentait** un gros ours. He said that his drawing **showed** a big bear.
> ➤ Nous ne savons pas ce que ça **représente**. We don't know what this **shows/depicts/illustrate**s.
> ➤ Le tableau **représentait** des valeurs morales. The painting **illustrated** moral values.
> ➤ Pour moi c'est une image qui **représente** la sérénité complète. To me it is a scene that **illustrates** complete serenity.

3 - To imagine

> ➤ Elle essaie de **se représenter** la cuisine peinte en bleu. She is trying **to imagine** the kitchen painted in blue.
> ➤ Il m'est difficile de **me représenter** ta mère en colère. It is difficult for me **to imagine** your mother angry.
> ➤ Tu **te représentes** une telle scène? Can you **imagine** such a spectacle?
> ➤ On **se représente** le désordre sans difficulté. It is not difficult to **imagine** the commotion.

4 - To crop up again, to happen again

> ➤ Espérons qu'une autre chance **se représentera** bientôt. Let's hope that another chance **will crop up** soon.
> ➤ Malheureusement l'occasion ne **s'est** jamais **représentée**. Unfortunately the opportunity never **cropped up again**.
> ➤ Tu penses vraiment que la même chose pourrait **se représenter**? Do you really think that the same thing could **happen again**?
> ➤ Si ça **se représente** je pars. If that **happens again** I am off.

5 - To perform (acting)

> ➤ Ils vont **représenter** devant des étudiants de toutes les nationalités. They are going **to perform** in front of students of all nationalities.

- ➤ Nous **aurons représenté** trois pièces en trois mois. We **will have performed** three plays in three months.
- ➤ Quand devez-vous **représenter** dans cette ville? When are you due **to perform** in that town?
- ➤ Ma classe voudrait **représenter** une pièce de cet auteur. My class would like **to perform** a play by this author.

6 - To resit an exam: reflexive form.

7 - To stand, to run (for election) again: reflexive form.

RETIRER - SE RETIRER

1 - To take off, to take away, to remove

- ➤ Il **avait retiré** ses lentilles. He **had taken off/had removed** his contact lenses.
- ➤ N'oublie pas de **retirer** ton collier. Don't forget **to take off/to remove** your necklace.
- ➤ Ça te **retire** la confiance une chose pareille n'est-ce pas. Such a thing **takes away** your confidence doesn't it.
- ➤ Vous n'allez pas les **retirer** du club maintenant! You can't possibly **take** them **away** from the club now!

2 - To withdraw

> ➢ On leur **a retiré** tous leurs privilèges. They had all their privileges **withdrawn**.
> ➢ Elle **a retiré** son nom de la liste de volontaires. She **withdrew** her name from the list of volunteers.
> ➢ Ils ont finalement **retiré** leur plainte. They finally **withdrew** their complaint.
> ➢ Je pense **retirer** ma démission. I am thinking about **withdrawing** my resignation.

3 - To collect, to pick up

> ➢ Nous **retirerons** nos valises de la consigne à quelle heure? We **will collect/will pick up** our suitcases at the left-luggage office at what time?
> ➢ Où doit-on **retirer** nos tickets pour le spectacle? Where do we **collect** our tickets for the show?
> ➢ Je dois **retirer** les documents à l'agence. I have **to collect/to pick up** the documents at the agency.
> ➢ Quelqu'un viendra **retirer** ce colis après cinq heures. Someone will come **to collect/to pick up** this parcel after five.

4 - To gain

- ➤ Une leçon pour tous **a été retirée** de cette expérience. We have all **gained** a lesson from that experience.
- ➤ Quels avantages **retirerait**-il? What advantages **would he gain**?
- ➤ Je n'**ai** absolument rien **retiré** de ce colloque. I **gained** absolutely nothing from this lecture.
- ➤ Que **retireriez**-vous d'un tel comportement? What **would** you **gain** by behaving like that?

5 - To retire, to withdraw

- ➤ Ils **se sont retirés** très tôt hier soir. They **retired** very early last night.
- ➤ J'ai l'intention de **me retirer** à la campagne. I intend **to retire** to the countryside.
- ➤ Il veut **se retirer** du monde. He wants **to retire** from the world.
- ➤ **Retirons**-nous dans mon bureau. Let's **retire** to my office.

RETOURNER - SE RETOURNER

1 - To return, to give back, to send back

- Ils leur **auraient retourné** le cadeau de mariage. They **would have returned/would have given back/would have sent** back the wedding present to them.
- Notre lettre **a été retournée**. Our letter **has been returned/has been sent back**.
- Je **retournerai** la visite bientôt. I **will return** the visit soon.
- Tu veux que nous te **retournions** les brochures? Did you want us **to give back/to send back** the brochures to you?

2 - To turn upside-down, to turn over, to turn inside out

- **Retourne** le tissu pour le repasser. **Turn** the material **upside-down** to iron it.
- Les assiettes **étaient retournées** sur l'évier. The plates **were turned upside-down** on the sink.
- Je **retourne** le matelas une fois par an. I **turn over** the mattress once a year.
- Et si nous **retournions** les sacs de couchage avant de les mettre au soleil? What about **turning** the sleeping bags **inside out** before putting them in the sun?

3 - To turn round

> Elle **s'est retournée** trois fois. She **turned round** three times.
> Nous l'avons vu **se retourner** tout à coup. We saw him **turn round** suddenly.
> Ne te **retourne** pas encore. Don't **turn round** yet.
> Ces images ont continué de **retourner** dans ma tête toute la nuit. Those images continued **to turn round** in my head the whole night.

4 - To go back, to return

> Quand **retournerons**-nous sur la Côte d'Azur? When **will** we **go back** to the Côte d'Azur?
> Je voudrais y **retourner** avant Pâques. I would like **to go back** there before Easter.
> Il a dit qu'il ne **retournera** plus dans ce magasin. He said that he **will** never **go back** to this shop.
> Elle y **est retournée** mardi dernier. She **went back/returned** there last Tuesday.

5 - To turn (to people)

> Il n'a personne sur qui **se retourner**. There is nobody he can **turn** to.

➢ Elle **s'est** toujours **retournée** sur sa grand-mère. She **has** always **turned** to her grandmother.

➢ Nous **nous sommes retournés** sur nos enfants. We **turned** to our children.

➢ Je sais que je peux toujours **me retourner** sur cette amie. I do know that I can **turn** to this friend any time.

6 - To shake, to upset, to move

➢ Le documentaire **l'a retourné**. The documentary **has shaken/has upset** him.

➢ Ça me **retourne** un animal qui souffre. It **upsets** me to see an animal in pain.

➢ Ton témoignage les **a** complètement **retournés**. Your experience **has** really **moved** them.

➢ Cette musique ne manque jamais de nous **retourner**. This music never fails **to move** us.

REVENIR

1 - To come back, to return

> ➢ Ils **sont revenus** après Noël. They **came back/returned** after Christmas.
> ➢ Vous **reviendrez** ensemble? **Will** you **come back** together?
> ➢ Nous **étions revenus** la veille. We **had come back/had returned** the day before.
> ➢ Quand vas-tu **revenir** ici? When are you going **to come back** here?

2 - To go back, to go over again

> ➢ Ils **sont revenus** sur la difficulté en question de mal gré. They reluctantly **went back** to the snag in question.
> ➢ Nous ne **reviendrons** pas sur ce point délicat. We **will** not **go over** that delicate argument **again**.
> ➢ Elle a refusé de **revenir** sur la première idée. She refused **to go over** the first idea **again**.
> ➢ Pourquoi **revenir** sur ça? Why **go over** that **again**?

3 - To go back (on one's word)

- ➤ Tu ne peux pas **revenir** sur ta promesse. You can't **go back** on your promise.
- ➤ Je ne **reviens** jamais sur ma parole. I never **go back** on my word.
- ➤ Elle n'a pas cru qu'il **était revenu** sur sa parole. She didn't believe that he **had gone back** on his word.
- ➤ Malheureusement il avait fallu qu'elles **reviennent** sur leur engagement. Sadly they had had **to go back** on their commitment.

4 - To pull through, to recover, to get over

- ➤ Nous avions abandonné tout espoir de la voir **revenir** de cette affreuse maladie. We had given up all hopes to see her **pull through** that awful illness.
- ➤ Est-ce qu'elle **est revenue** de la nouvelle? Has she **recovered** from the news?
- ➤ C'est un de ces chocs dont on ne **revient** pas. You never **get over** a blow like that.
- ➤ Il n'en **revient** pas. He can't **get over** it.

5 - To amount (to), to come down (to), to achieve

> Voilà à quoi cela **est revenu**. That is what it **amounted/came down** to.
> Tout ceci **revient** à une question de principe. This all **comes down** to a question of principle.
> Cela **revient** à la même chose n'est-ce pas? It **amounts/comes down** to the same thing doesn't it?
> Ça **reviendrait** à quoi? What **would** it **achieve**?

6 - To cost, to be (a price)

> Les frais annuels pour une voiture comme ça **reviendraient** trop chers. The annual cost for a car like that **would be** too high.
> Ça vous **est revenu** à combien? How much **did** it **cost** you?
> Les dépenses vont **revenir** à environ 2 000 €. The expenses are going **to be** about 2000 €.
> De telles transformations **reviendraient** beaucoup trop cher pour nous. Such alterations **would cost** too much for us.

7 - To belong/fall (to people, with 'rights' or 'responsibility' as subjects).

ROULER - SE ROULER

1 - To roll, to roll up

- ➢ Le chien **se roulait** dans l'herbe. The dog **was rolling** in the grass.
- ➢ Nos fillettes **se sont roulées** dans le sable. Our little girls **rolled** in the sand.
- ➢ Mon grand-père aimait **rouler** ses cigarettes. My grandfather used to enjoy **rolling** his cigarettes.
- ➢ Nous **avions roulé** le tapis. We **had rolled up** the carpet.

2 - To go (transport), to drive

- ➢ Puis le train s'est mis à **rouler** de plus en plus lentement. Then the train started **to go** slower and slower.
- ➢ Il **roulait** beaucoup trop vite dans le brouillard. He **was going/was driving** much too fast in the fog.
- ➢ On **a roulé** toute la nuit. We **drove** all night.
- ➢ N'oublie pas de **rouler** à droite. Don't forget **to drive** on the right.

3 - To diddle

> ➢ Ils ne peuvent s'empêcher **de rouler** les touristes. They can't help **diddling** tourists.
> ➢ Je n'**ai** jamais **roulé** personne. I **have** never **diddled** anyone.
> ➢ On vous **a roulé**? **Did** they **diddle** you?
> ➢ Le client **a été roulé**. The customer **has been diddled**.

4 - To wheel/roll along (things on wheels).

SAUVER - SE SAUVER

1 - To save, to rescue, to salvage

> ➢ Nous **avons été sauvés** juste à temps. We **were saved/were rescued** just in time.
> ➢ Ils essaient de **sauver** le chat du trou depuis deux heures. They have been trying **to rescue** the cat from the hole for two hours.

- ➤ Malgré les très grandes vagues le petit garçon a pu **être sauvé**. Despite the very big waves the little boy **was saved/was rescued**.
- ➤ Qu'avez-vous pu **sauver** de l'inondation? What have you been able **to save/to salvage** from the flood?

2 - To run away, to escape

- ➤ J'ai vu trois gamins **se sauver** par là. I saw three young boys **running away** in that direction.
- ➤ Vous aviez décidé de **vous sauver** pendant la nuit? Had you decided **to run away** during the night?
- ➤ Le prisonnier **s'est sauvé** pour la deuxième fois. The prisoner **escaped** for the second time.
- ➤ Elle n'est pas arrivée à **se sauver**. She didn't manage **to run away/to escape**.

3 - To get going, to go, to leave, to be off

- ➤ **Sauve-toi** ou tu vas encore être en retard. **Get going/go/be off** or you are going to be late again.
- ➤ Il faut que nous **nous sauvions** si nous ne voulons pas manquer le bus. We must **get going/go/leave/be off** if we don't want to miss the bus.
- ➤ Pourquoi **s'est**-il **sauvé** quand tu es arrivé? Why **did** you **go/leave** when you arrived?
- ➤ Pas la peine de **vous sauver** à cause de moi. There is no need **to go/to leave** because of me.

SENTIR - SE SENTIR

1 - To smell

- ➤ Ça **sentait** mauvais dans la caravane hier. It **smelled** horrible in the caravan yesterday.
- ➤ **Sentez** ces fleurs. **Smell** these flowers.
- ➤ Tu **sens** la lavande. You **smell** of lavender.
- ➤ Je **sens** de la fumée dans le jardin. I can **smell** smoke in the garden.

2 - To feel

- ➤ Comment **se sent** votre mère maintenant? How **does** your mother **feel** now?
- ➤ Il faisait si froid qu'il ne **sentait** plus ses doigts. It was so cold that he couldn't **feel** his fingers any more.
- ➤ Elle **s'est sentie** mal après le repas. She **felt** unwell after the meal.
- ➤ Je **me sens** de mieux en mieux. I **feel** better and better.

3 - To be aware of, to feel

- ➢ On **sentait** de la résistance parmi le groupe. We **were aware** of some resistance amongst the group.
- ➢ Je **sens** que tu n'es pas d'accord. I **am aware/feel** that you don't agree.
- ➢ Nous **sentions** que ça finirait mal. We **felt** that it would end in tears.
- ➢ Il **a senti** qu'il leur avait fait de la peine. He **was aware/felt** that he had hurt them.

SOULEVER - SE SOULEVER

1 - To lift

- ➢ Qui **a soulevé** le couvercle de la casserole? Who **has lifted** the lid off the saucepan?
- ➢ Nous n'avons pas pu **soulever** la coiffeuse. We couldn't **lift** the dressing table.
- ➢ Je ne dois rien **soulever** pendant six semaines. I mustn't **lift** anything for six weeks.
- ➢ Elle **soulevait** le voilage pour mieux voir. She **used to lift** the net curtain so that she could see better.

2 - To trigger, to cause, to bring, to raise

- ➢ C'est ça qui **a soulevé** la colère chez ses employés. That is what **triggered** anger amongst his/her employees.
- ➢ La remarque **a soulevé** une gêne générale dans la salle. The comment **caused/brought** general embarrassment in the hall.
- ➢ C'est une personne qui **soulève** l'enthousiasme autour d'elle. She is someone who **brings** enthusiasm to all around her.
- ➢ Cela **avait soulevé** beaucoup de doutes parmi les abonnés. That **had raised** a great deal of doubts amongst the subscribers.

TENIR - SE TENIR

1 - To hold

> Ils se promenaient en **se tenant** la main. They were walking **holding** hands.
> Tu veux que je **tienne** le miroir? Do you want me **to hold** the mirror for you?
> Le nœud n'**a** pas **tenu**. The knot **did** not **hold**.
> Qu'est-ce qu'il **tenait**? What **was** he **holding**?

2 - To keep

> Il est obligatoire de **tenir** les chiens en laisse dans le parc. It is compulsory **to keep** dogs on the lead in the park.
> Je **tiendrai** les pizzas au chaud pour eux. I **will keep** the pizzas hot for them.
> Il **tient** son jardin comme un professionnel. He **keeps** his garden like a professional would.
> Il est essentiel que la piscine **soit tenue** propre. It is vital that the swimming pool **is kept** clean.

2 - To insist, to feel strongly about

- ➤ Il **a tenu** à nous aider. He **insisted** that he helps us.
- ➤ Elle **avait tenu** à payer. She **had insisted** that she should pay.
- ➤ Ils **tiennent** à revenir avant la naissance du bébé. They **feel strongly about** coming back before the birth of the baby.
- ➤ Nous **tenons** beaucoup à ces photos. We really **feel strongly** about these photos.

3 - To run (a business), to hold (a business)

- ➤ Mon parrain et ma marraine **tiennent** une quincaillerie depuis vingt ans. My godfather and godmother **have been running** a hardware shop for twenty years.
- ➤ Je voudrais bien **tenir** une boutique pour adolescents. I would love **to run** a boutique for teenagers.
- ➤ Un couple anglais **tient** le gîte. An English couple **runs** the gîte.
- ➤ Vous allez **tenir** un étal au marché? Are you going **to hold** a stall at the market?

4 - To have, to get

- ➤ Elle **tenait** une sale grippe depuis deux semaines. She **had had** a dreaful bout of flu for two weeks.

> ➤ Il **tient** un gros rhume chaque hiver. He **has/gets** a big cold every winter.
> ➤ Elle **tient** ce renseignement de sa voisine. She **has/gets** this information from her neighbour.
> ➤ Il **tient** sa passion pour le sport de son père. He **gets** his keenness for sport from his father.

5 - To behave

> ➤ Ils **se sont** mal **tenus** au baptême. They **behaved** badly at the christening.
> ➤ **Tiens-toi** bien! **Behave yourself.**
> ➤ Elle m'a demandé si vous **vous étiez** mieux **tenus** que la dernière fois. She has asked me whether you **behaved** better than last time.
> ➤ Comment **se sont**-elles **tenues** pendant le cours? How **did** they **behave** during the lesson?

6 - To regard/consider (as something or someone).

7 - To be (still) on (arrangements).

8 - To take after (people).

9 - To be held, to take place: reflexive form.

10 - To fit (into a space).

TOUCHER - SE TOUCHER

1 - To touch

> J'ai voulu **toucher** le manteau en fourrure. I wanted **to touch** the fur coat.

> Tu **as** encore **touché** tes boutons? **Did** you **touch** your spots again?

> Elle ne veut pas qu'on **touche** aux décorations de son gâteau. She doesn't want us **to touch** the decorations on her cake.

> Il ne faut pas que les boîtes **se touchent**. The boxes mustn't **touch**.

2 - To concern, to affect

> Nos nouvelles le **toucheront**. Our news **will concern/will affect** him.

> Dans les circonstances je me suis senti **touché**. I did feel **concerned/affected** in the circumstances.

> Tout cela ne vous **touche** pas du tout. All that does not **concern/affect** you at all.

> Sa mort les **avait** profondément **touchés**. His/her death **had** deeply **affected** them.

3 - To hit

- ➤ Le ballon m'**a touché** à la jambe droite. The ball **hit** my right leg.
- ➤ Il **a été touché** en plein cœur. He **was hit** in the heart.
- ➤ Heureusement la pierre ne m'**a** pas **touché**. Fortunately the stone **did** not **hit** me.
- ➤ Où **as**-tu **été touché**? Where **were** you **hit**?

4 - To get (money)

- ➤ Combien **touche**-t-il pour sa retraite? How much **does** he **get** from his retirement fund?
- ➤ Nous n'**avons** rien **touché**. We **did** not **get** anything (any money).
- ➤ Je vais **toucher** une prime à Noël. I am going **to get** a bonus at Christmas.
- ➤ Elle ne **touche** que 100 € par semaine. She only **gets** 100 € a week.

5 - To get in touch with, to contact.

6 - To meddle/tamper with.

TRAITER - SE TRAITER

1 - To treat

> Il ne veut pas qu'ils **soient traités** durement. He doesn't want them **to be treated** severely.
> Elle **traite** les animaux de la même manière qu'elle **traite** les êtres humains. She **treats** animals in the same way as she **treats** human beings.
> On **traitera** l'affaire avec beaucoup de patience. We **will treat** the issue with a lot of patience.
> C'est comme ça que vous me **traitez** aujourd'hui? Is that how you **treat** me today?

2 - To welcome, to entertain

> Nous **traiterons** ton ami comme un fils. We **will welcome** your friend as our own son.
> Elle m'**a** bien **traité** chaque fois que j'y suis allé. She really **welcomed** me every time I went there.
> Tu n'aurais pas pu les **traiter** un peu mieux? Couldn't you have **welcomed/entertained** them a bit better?
> Je me demande comment il va **traiter** ses beaux-parents. I wonder how he is going **to entertain/welcome** his in-laws.

3 - To deal with, to handle

- ➤ Comment va-t-il **traiter** la nouvelle situation? How is he going **to deal with/handle** the new situation?
- ➤ La presse **a traité** ce scandale avec objectivité à mon avis. The press **dealt with/handled** this scandal objectively in my opinion.
- ➤ Il est impossible que vous **ayez traité** le sujet en connaissance de cause. It is not possible that you **have dealt with/handled** the matter with full knowledge of the facts.
- ➤ Ce n'est pas le propos que nous voulons **traiter** pour le moment. That is not the subject we want **to deal with** just now.

4 - To call (someone names)

- ➤ Il les **a traités** de voyous. He **called** them thugs.
- ➤ Vous **vous êtes traités** de paresseux? **Did** you **call each other** lazy?
- ➤ Elle m'**a traité** de menteur. She **called** me a liar.
- ➤ C'est toi qui nous **traite** d'hypocrites! I don't believe you of all people **call** us hypocrites!

USER - S'USER

1 - To wear out/away, to use up

> Tu vas **t'user** les yeux si tu n'allumes pas la lumière.
> You are going **to wear** your eyes **out** if you don't
> switch the light on.
> Les soucis l'**ont usé**. Worries **have worn** him **out**.
> Ce sac **est** trop **usé**. This bag **is** too **worn out**.
> Qui **a usé** mon déodorant? Who **has used up** my
> deodorant?

2 - To use, to need

> Vous **usez** combien d'électricité par mois en moyenne?
> How much electricity **do** you **use** a month on average?
> On n'**use** que du charbon pour le feu de cheminée. We
> only **use** coal on the open fire.
> Quelle essence **use**-t-elle pour la tondeuse? What petrol
> **does** she **need** for the lawn mower?
> Ils **usent** trop d'eau. They **use/need** too much water.

VERSER - SE VERSER

1 - To pour

> Ensuite **versez** la sauce sur les pâtes. Next you **pour** the sauce on the pasta.
> Le champagne **était** déjà **versé** pour tout le monde. The champagne **was** already **poured** out for everyone.
> Attention cette carafe **verse** plutôt mal. Be careful this jug doesn't **pour** very well.
> **Versons-nous** un bon verre de limonade. **Let's pour ourselves** a lovely glass of lemonade.

2 - To pay

> Pourriez-vous **verser** des arrhes? Could you **pay** a deposit?
> Il lui **versait** une pension alimentaire. He **used to pay** him/her an allowance for food.
> Les allocations familiales vous **seront versées** à partir de janvier. Social security benefits **will be paid** to you from January.
> Quelle somme dois-je **verser**? How much do I have **to pay**?

3 - To shed (blood or tears), to spill (blood or tears)

- ➢ Trop de sang **a été versé**. Too much blood **has been shed**.
- ➢ Ne **verse** plus de sang pour lui. Don't **shed** any more blood for him.
- ➢ Je n'**ai** pas **versé** une seule larme pour lui. I **did** not **shed** a single tear for him.
- ➢ Si tu savais combien de larmes nous **avons versé** pour toi. If only you knew how many tears we **have shed** for you.

VOLER

1 - To steal, to rob

- ➤ Qu'est-ce qui **a été volé**? What **has been stolen**?
- ➤ Il **a volé** une grande somme d'argent à ses parents. He **stole** a large amount of money from his parents.
- ➤ Mon appareil-photo **a été volé**. My camera **has been stolen**.
- ➤ Vous **voliez** pour vivre? **Did** you **use to steal** in order to survive?

2 - To fly

- ➤ Je regardais les oiseaux **voler**. I used to watch the birds **fly**.
- ➤ L'avion **volait** au dessus des nuages. The plane **was flying** above the clouds.
- ➤ Il lui semblait qu'elle pourrait **voler**. She felt as though she could **fly**.
- ➤ La vitre **a volé** en éclats. The window **flew** into small pieces.

APPENDIX: CONVERSATIONAL VERBS

PRESENT	PAST	PRESENT	PAST
INFINITIVE		PARTICIPLE	
Abaisser	avoir abaissé	abaissant	abaissé, abaissée
Aboutir	avoir abouti	aboutissant	abouti, aboutie
Accepter	avoir accepté	acceptant	accepté, acceptée
Achever	avoir achevé	achevant	achevé, achevée
Adhérer	avoir adhéré	adhérant	adhéré, adhérée
Admettre	avoir admis	admettant	admis, admise
Agir	avoir agi	agissant	agi
Aller	être allé	allant	allé, allée
Apprendre	avoir appris	apprenant	appris, apprise
Appuyer	avoir appuyé	appuyant	appuyé, appuyée
Arracher	avoir arraché	arrachant	arraché, arrachée
Arranger	avoir arrangé	arrangeant	arrangé, arrangée
Arriver	être arrivé	arrivant	arrivé, arrivée
Assurer	avoir assuré	assurant	assuré, assurée
Avancer	avoir avancé	avançant	avancé, avancée
Bâiller	avoir bâillé	bâillant	bâillé
Balancer	avoir balancé	balançant	balancé, balancée
Bondir	avoir bondi	bondissant	bondi
Boucler	avoir bouclé	bouclant	bouclé, bouclée
Brouiller	avoir brouillé	brouillant	brouillé, brouillée
Causer	avoir causé	causant	causé, causée
Céder	avoir cédé	cédant	cédé, cédée
Charger	avoir chargé	chargeant	chargé, chargée
Combler	avoir comblé	comblant	comblé, comblée
Commander	avoir commandé	commandant	commandé, commandée
Composer	avoir composé	composant	composé, composée
Comprendre	avoir compris	comprenant	compris, comprise
Compter	avoir compté	comptant	compté, comptée
Confondre	avoir confondu	confondant	confondu, confondue
Convenir	avoir convenu	convenant	convenu, convenue

Craquer	avoir craqué	craquant	craqué, craquée
Déboucher	avoir débouché	débouchant	débouché, débouchée
Débrouiller	avoir débrouillé	débrouillant	débrouillé, débrouillée
Décharger	avoir déchargé	déchargeant	déchargé, déchargée
Décoller	avoir décollé	décollant	décollé, décollée
Découvrir	avoir découvert	découvrant	découvert, découverte
Défendre	avoir défendu	défendant	défendu, défendue
Dégager	avoir dégagé	dégageant	dégagé, dégagée
Dérouler	avoir déroulé	déroulant	déroulé, déroulée
Descendre	avoir descendu être descendu	descendant	descendu, descendue
Devoir	avoir dû	devant	dû, due
Dire	avoir dit	disant	dit, dite
Diriger	avoir dirigé	dirigeant	dirigé, dirigée
Disparaître	avoir disparu	disparaissant	disparu, disparue
Disposer	avoir disposé	disposant	disposé, disposée
Doubler	avoir doublé	doublant	doublé, doublée
Dresser	avoir dressé	dressant	dressé, dressée
Élever	avoir élevé	élevant	élevé, élevée
Emprunter	avoir emprunté	empruntant	emprunté, empruntée
Engager	avoir engagé	engageant	engagé, engagée
Entendre	avoir entendu	entendant	entendu. entendue
Entraîner	avoir entraîné	entraînant	entraîné, entraînée
Entretenir	avoir entretenu	entretenant	entretenu, entretenue
Estimer	avoir estimé	estimant	estimé, estimée
Ficher	avoir OR fiché être fichu	fichant	fiché, fichée fichu, fichue
Figurer	avoir figuré	figurant	figuré, figurée
Former	avoir formé	formant	formé, formée
Fuir	avoir fui	fuyant	fui
Gagner	avoir gagné	gagnant	gagné, gagnée
Garder	avoir gardé	gardant	gardé, gardée
Gêner	avoir gêné	gênant	gêné, gênée
Heurter	avoir heurté	heurtant	heurté, heurtée
Ignorer	avoir ignoré	ignorant	ignoré, ignorée
Importer	avoir importé	important	importé, importée

Introduire	avoir introduit	introduisant	introduit. introduite
Joindre	avoir joint	joignant	joint, jointe
Lâcher	avoir lâché	lâchant	lâché, lâchée
Lancer	avoir lancé	lançant	lancé, lancée
Livrer	avoir livré	livrant	livré, livrée
Louer	avoir loué	louant	loué, louée
Marcher	avoir marché	marchant	marché
Mettre	avoir mis	mettant	mis, mise
Mijoter	avoir mijoté	mijotant	mijoté, mijotée
Monter	avoir monté être monté	montant	monté, montée
Noter	avoir noté	notant	noté, notée
Noyer	avoir noyé	noyant	noyé, noyée
Obliger	avoir obligé	obligeant	obligé, obligée
Offrir	avoir offert	offrant	offert, offerte
Opérer	avoir opéré	opérant	opéré, opérée
Ordonner	avoir ordonné	ordonnant	ordonné, ordonnée
Parcourir	avoir parcouru	parcourant	parcouru, parcourue
Passer	avoir passé être passé	passant	passé, passée
Placer	avoir placé	plaçant	placé, placée
Plaindre	avoir plaint	plaignant	plaint, plainte
Planter	avoir planté	plantant	planté, plantée
Porter	avoir porté	portant	porté, portée
Poser	avoir posé	posant	posé, posée
Poursuivre	avoir poursuivi	poursuivant	poursuivi, poursuivie
Pousser	avoir poussé	poussant	poussé, poussée
Prendre	avoir pris	prenant	pris, prise
Presser	avoir pressé	pressant	pressé, pressée
Rappeler	avoir rappelé	rappelant	rappelé, rappelée
Rapporter	avoir rapporté	rapportant	rapporté, rapportée
Rattraper	avoir rattrapé	rattrapant	rattrapé, rattrapée
Recueillir	avoir recueilli	recueillant	recueilli, recueillie
Récupérer	avoir récupéré	récupérant	récupéré, récupérée
Regarder	avoir regardé	regardant	regardé, regardée
Régler	avoir réglé	réglant	réglé, réglée

Rejeter	avoir rejeté	rejetant	rejeté. rejetée
Relever	avoir relevé	relevant	relevé, relevée
Remettre	avoir remis	remettant	remis, remise
Remonter	avoir remonté être remonté	remontant	remonté, remontée
Rendre	avoir rendu	rendant	rendu, rendue
Renverser	avoir renversé	renversant	renversé, renversée
Repasser	avoir repassé être repassé	repassant	repassé, repassée
Reporter	avoir reporté	reportant	reporté, reportée
Reposer	avoir reposé	reposant	reposé, reposée
Représenter	avoir représenté	représentant	représenté, représentée
Retirer	avoir retiré	retirant	retiré, retirée
Retourner	avoir retourné être retourné	retournant	retourné, retournée
Revenir	être revenu	revenant	revenu, revenue
Rouler	avoir roulé	roulant	roulé, roulée
Sauver	avoir sauvé	sauvant	sauvé, sauvée
Sentir	avoir senti	sentant	senti, sentie
Soulever	avoir soulevé	soulevant	soulevé, soulevée
Tenir	avoir tenu	tenant	tenu, tenue
Toucher	avoir touché	touchant	touché, touchée
Traiter	avoir traité	traitant	traité, traitée
User	avoir usé	usant	usé, usée
Verser	avoir versé	versant	versé, versée
Voler	avoir volé	volant	volé, volée

NOTE 1 - Compound tenses of reflexive verbs are conjugated with **être.**

NOTE 2 - Where **avoir** and **être** can both function as the auxiliary verb, generally **avoir** is used when the main verb is used transitively and **être** is used when the main verb is used intransitively. However there are some exceptions to this general rule.

HADLEY PAGER INFO PUBLICATIONS
French-English, English-French

HADLEY'S CONVERSATIONAL FRENCH PHRASE BOOK
Paperback, 1997, 256 pages, 148 x 105 mm
ISBN 1-872739-05-9   Price: £6.00
♦ Over 2000 French/English phrases and 2000 English/French phrases
♦ Eleven conversational topic vocabularies ♦ Aide-memoire key-word dictionary

HADLEY'S FRENCH MOTORING PHRASE BOOK & DICTIONARY
Paperback, 2001, 176 pages, 148 x 105 mm
ISBN 1-872739-09-1   Price: £6.00
♦ Asking the Way, Road Signs, Car Hire, Parking, Breakdowns, Accidents, Types of Vehicle, Cycling and Motor Sports. ♦ Extensive Dictionary   ♦ Over 3000 words and phrases included

HADLEY'S FRENCH MEDICAL PHRASE BOOK
Paperback, 2004, 160 pages, 148 x 105 mm
ISBN 1-872739-13-X   Price: £6.00
♦ At the Doctor's, At the Hospital, Baby's, Children's, Young People's, Male, Female Health. Also At the Chemist, At the Dentist, At the Optician's, Accidents & Emergencies ♦ Reference Section: Baby's Requirements, Common Illnesses, The Body

GLOSSARY OF FRENCH LEGAL TERMS
Paperback, 1999, 114 pages, 210 x 148 mm
ISBN 1-872739-07-5   Price: £12.00
♦ Provides over 4000 French legal words and phrases associated with legislation falling within the Civil Code and the Penal Code, (eg house purchase and wills), but company and commercial legislation is not covered.

The above publications are available through good booksellers or can be obtained directly from Hadley Pager Info by sending a cheque to cover the price (postage is free within the UK, add 10% if outside the UK) to **Hadley Pager Info, PO Box 249, Leatherhead, KT23 3WX, England**. Latest Publication List available on request.
Website: www.hadleypager.com   Email: hpinfo@aol..com

HADLEY PAGER INFO PUBLICATIONS
French-English, English-French

GLOSSARY OF HOUSE PURCHASE AND RENOVATION TERMS
Paperback, 2000, Fourth Edition, 56 pages, 210 x 148 mm
ISBN 1-872739-08-3   Price: £7.50
♦ Provides over 2000 French words and phrases used by estate agents, notaires, mortgage lenders, builders, decorators, etc.

CONCISE DICTIONARY OF HOUSE BUILDING (Arranged by Trades)
Paperback, 2001, Second Edition, 256 pages, 210 x 144 mm
ISBN 1-872739-11-3 Price £27.00
♦ Dictionary is divided into 14 Sections covering various stages and trades employed in house building □ Over 10,000 terms in each language

GLOSSARY OF GARDENING AND HORTICULTURAL TERMS
Paperback, 2004, Third Edition, 72 pages, 210 x 145 mm
ISBN 1-872739-14-8   Price: £8.50
♦ Glossary includes close to 2000 gardening and horticultural terms, which cover the majority of garden plants and shrubs, as well as fruit, trees, herbs, vegetables, procedures, equipment, pests, etc. ♦Appendices of Butterflies, Birds and Medicinal Plants.

GLOSSARY OF MEDICAL, HEALTH AND PHARMACY TERMS
Paperback, 2003, 204 pages, 210 x 148 mm
ISBN 1-872739-12-1   Price: £12.50
♦ An up-to-date source of over 3000 medical, health and pharmacy terms covering a wide range of common illnesses and diseases, anatomical terms, first-aid and hospital terms, as well as pharmacy terms embracing medicines, toiletries, cosmetics, health and pharmaceutical products

The above publications are available through good booksellers or can be obtained directly from Hadley Pager Info by sending a cheque to cover the price (postage is free within the UK, add 10% if outside the UK) to **Hadley Pager Info, PO Box 249, Leatherhead, KT23 3WX, England**. Latest Publication List available on request.
Website: www.hadleypager.com   Email: hpinfo@aol.com